Ros Ball and James Millar are both journalists working in politics in Westminster. They live in south London with their two children.

ROS BALL & JAMES MILLAR

THE GENDER POLICE: A DIARY

With thanks to Simon Vaughan and Anna Auckland

Contents

Foreword

After giving a lecture to law students at a German university I found myself in a round of students and young lawyers - females and males. They were brilliant young people. Of course I expected sophisticated questions on legal problems, but none came.

Instead, a woman started the discussion with the question, "Are you Ms....., the author of the book 'There's a good girl'? You should know that I was raised according to your book. I remember very well that it was always in the kitchen at home and my mother reread it whenever she had time". A male student related the same tale. His mother kept the book beside her bed. They started a discussion on gender problems instead of legal issues.

I was expecting criticism, but none came, they agreed with my attempt at a gender-neutral upbringing and assured me that they were happy with the way their parents had guided them to be 'different' from stereotyped gender role models. And as a result, as I could see at the event, females and males equal in numbers and in their professional positions - in their first employment.

Reading Ros' and James' diary it seems to me that ostensibly things have not changed in 30 years, when it comes to the 'blue and pink', the 'tough man and princess' questions. Nevertheless daily life for young women has changed for the better and young men are starting to pay more attention to family and their kids and are emphasising 'the great career' less – as they were still expected to do one generation before. Statistics in Germany substantiate this trend.

A company employing a generative young guy who is becoming a father can't be sure that he won't ask for

9

paternity leave or part-time work. Not so long ago these things were connected only to women of reproductive age and hereby exacerbated disadvantages in employment.

But I am perplexed: On the one hand, comparing both diaries obviously nothing had changed in turning a child of female sex into a 'good girl' and a child of male sex into a 'real boy'. All these little stories of a child demanding for this or that, just to be like a girl, a boy, a woman, a man… like all the others, left me bewildered and threw me back 30 years.

How should this polarity be dissolved?

I tried to explain in 1984 why children stick to the role model of 'pink' and 'blue' perseveringly, they wish to be like everybody else to become a proper member of society, to be like 'all other adults'.

In the process of a child's growing up we teach them in many other fields to behave in the way life in 'our' society demands: how to wash hands, to use the toilet, to dress, to use a knife and fork, to be polite, to read and write, to study busily to become a successful person in life. Their duty is to focus on copying the adults' behaviour. We thump it into their brain. And why the hell should it be different for gender issues? How to explain the difference to a 3-year-old? I think it is not as much how parents individually guide their children, it is more the issue of the overall impression in our society and the behaviour of both genders in practice.

It will be different in future when not only gender-daddy and gender-mummy are different but also all other adults as seen in advertising, on TV, in politics, in movies, toys and in reality in their jobs.

I had the chance to give a lecture to 10-year-olds in primary school on my specific field in law as a judge. When they had written down their conclusions on what they learnt, one girl's result was, "Originally I planned to become a movie actress, but now I changed my mind definitely, I will become a judge".

It is time for women to go into politics and well paid jobs more than ever with the intention to alter role models. Furthermore, women should be aware in selecting their future job that they will earn enough to support a family – including gender-daddy. By the way, in more and more young couples she is the one who earns more money than he.

It is time for men to stay at home to alter male role models. Females should stay away from the mirror and from domestic chores.

Margaret Mead, the famous American anthropologist in the thirties, told her daughter, "If you cannot abide the dust under the bed you will never be successful in your research" and Christiane Nüßlein-Volhard, a German awarded the Nobel Prize for Biology, said, "Women should spend less time in front of the mirror but more time with the microscope".

Maybe in 2045 we will have another diary to see if there are any improvements. But even Rome was not built in a day.

Persistence means altering little things steadily. So keep up the good work!

Marianne Grabrucker

Author, *There's a Good Girl: Gender Stereotyping in the First Three Years – A Diary* (1985)

Preface

Woop woop it's the gender police. Woop woop, they're everywhere but it's hard to see them. You may even be one of them – but you're such a secret agent even you don't know you are.

We'd always been dimly aware of the gender police, but it was having children that brought the idea into sharp focus. In 2007 our daughter was born, and a frustration with the pink and blue divide erupted in us. When our son was born in 2010, it was a second hand 1980's book from eBay that helped us make sense of that frustration. That book, *There's a Good Girl: Gender Stereotyping in the First Three Years - A Diary* by German lawyer Marianne Grabrucker, had a significant effect on our lives as parents.

The book is based around a simple but brilliant idea; if you start to make a daily note of the way the world 'polices' a child by gender, you have a record of how girls and boys are not born equal. If they do behave differently, this book gave us some answers as to why. Our kids weren't born different, it was the world around them that was treating them differently. The way people spoke to them and the language they used, the toys and clothes they gave them, and the expectations they had of them – they were enforcing certain gender roles, they were policing their behaviour.

When someone experiences problems at work they are often told to keep a diary as a record, possibly to be used as a body of evidence in a tribunal. Grabrucker's diary had the same sort of power. It compiled the everyday complaint or anecdote into a bigger picture, rather than a jumble of frustrated feelings that something is not right. She notes the effect on her daughter of billboards on the street, casual

13

comments from strangers, and the way other children enforce their understanding of their roles as a boy or girl on their peers.

Grabrucker also examined her own behaviour towards her daughter and found that parents are by no means excepted from this issue, much as they might want to think themselves enlightened.

The book inspired us to start keeping our own Twitter diary about our 3-year-old girl and our baby boy and how people treated them differently. We hoped things had improved since the 80s, but we weren't sure how our experience would be different. The first major change was the way we were able to publish our diary on Twitter every day, to connect with people who were similarly interested in this problem, but also to discuss ways of helping us all to break out of these stereotypes. The other difference is that this is written by both mother *and* father and is about stereotypes of both girls *and* boys. Though we come from a firmly feminist position, what we've learnt is that things haven't changed enough since Gloria Steinem said,

"We've begun to raise daughters more like sons... but few have the courage to raise our sons more like our daughters."

The diary is a mish-mash of angry reactions, disappointment with the world and righteous indignation (not always deployed sensibly, but that's the immediacy of social media for you). But it's also peppered with humour, discussion, and ways we tried to push against something that we don't agree with.

We hope it helps you to think about the ways you were treated as a child, and the way you treat children now. We certainly didn't write it to openly criticise anyone's parenting – more often than not we learnt about our own behaviour – our aim was just to expose the thin veneer of equality around us all. It can seem invisible at times, but we hope that if you can see it, you'll want to change it too.

Ros Ball and James Millar

March 2015

The Diary

The diary is reprinted here from our Twitter feed @GenderDiary with some corrections, edits and swapping text-speak for real words.

10th January 2011

This account is inspired by Marianne Grabrucker's *There's a Good Girl: Gender Stereotyping in the First Three Years - A Diary*. Things happen to our children on a daily basis that make us aware of sex-role conditioning but to which so many people seem oblivious. We'll be tweeting about everyday things that people say and do that seem to confirm gender consciousness to our children.

Taken to the panto by her granny this weekend our daughter and her cousins were buying toys at a stall. Her two older male cousins said, "Why don't you get this?" and directed her to the pink fluffy tiara. One of her male cousins chose a flashing torch which had pink plastic casing. The woman on the stall said, "Shall I get you that in blue?"

11th January 2011

Being shown round her new nursery a member of staff said to our daughter, "This is what we call the boys corner". It's a play table for cars.

One of my nephews started school yesterday. His mum couldn't find his hairbrush to comb his messy curly hair. His older brother laughed at him and said he looked "like a girl".

17

12th January 2011

This quote from Marianne Grabrucker sums it up well, "Children are classified as being typical or untypical of their sex... human behaviour, with varying natural talents and preferences, does not exist."

At a baby clinic getting our baby boy weighed today. I notice how the health visitors praise heavy boy babies, "Isn't he a lovely big boy?" Both our children have been at the heavy end of the scale but I haven't heard my girl or other people's being called "a lovely big girl". It's possible some people wouldn't like their girl to be called big in size. We refer to girls as big when they are being "grown up". I have a friend whose pet name for her son is 'Big boy'. She doesn't call her daughter 'Big girl'.

Evidence based research shows that of babies rated by their parents at no more than 24 hours old, girls were perceived to have finer features, boys were perceived to be bigger, stronger and better co-ordinated. But there were actually no overall differences between the babies. It's possible boys are handled more roughly from the day they are born for this reason.

13th January 2011

Third day of tweeting was a quiet day. Only thing to report that was odd is daughter saying when the baby gurgles, "That's like a girl". When asked what a boy baby sounds like she says a boy cries and that happy noises are "like a girl". No idea what this means.

Also want to add a couple of back-dated things. A comment

from a shop assistant in a shoe shop when our daughter was 2 and was climbing around with her nappy showing from under her skirt, "Don't show everyone that. That's your special secret". Repeat: 2 and in nappies.

14th January 2011

Today we had visitors. Our daughter wanted to wear a bridesmaid's dress she had worn for a friend's wedding. She said she wanted to wear her dress because the visitors "will like me". She was right I suppose. A girl in a frilly dress gets a lot of, "Don't you look lovely in your pretty dress!" etc. She obviously associates people appreciating her appearance with being liked. There isn't much discussion from visitors about what our boy is wearing or how pretty he looks.

15th January 2011

A friend told me about a little boy she knows who likes dressing up in necklaces, hats and handbags. She isn't very comfortable with this. Although girls' and boys' toys and games are often gender segregated, girls have more freedom to play with so called 'boys' toys. The friend has a baby boy herself. Like a vast majority of parents of boys, she won't be encouraging dressing up games that are 'for girls'. I wonder what the fear is for the sons who might play dressing up in necklaces. The fact being called a girl is an insult says a lot.

16th January 2011

A little more clarity from the 3-year-old on why her baby brother is "like a girl". She says it's because "only girls smile". Tempted to assume that this might be to do with adverts and general cultural messages about women's appearances. But who knows.

17th January 2011

Just picked up our eldest from nursery. All the boys were sitting at one table with cars and trucks. All the girls on the floor with a game. I have heard the staff reinforce this behaviour before. Some might claim the children's behaviour informs the adult response, but how can you prove which came first? Staff also encouraged our daughter to "come and play with the girls" on her first day.

20th January 2011

Keeping this diary we've got to be honest about how we might be treating our boy and girl differently as well. Clothes are where we really can't escape social convention without making a big statement. Our boy is in purple today but mostly he's in the standard blue and sludge brown colours. All hand-me-down clothes come ready sorted by gender but it's the one area where very few people dare to tread – putting boys in 'girl' colours. Would like to hear if anyone has seen otherwise. Again it seems more socially acceptable for girls to wear 'boys' clothes/colours. Why is it so unacceptable for boys to be like girls at all?

21st January 2011

At the doctors, a friendly old gentleman asks if the baby is a boy. He says how nice it is that we have one of each then tells me, "It's good because one day he'll be able to do your decorating and she'll be able to cook for you." I point out that in our house Dad is a good cook and Mum is good at woodwork. He immediately tells me that his son-in-law does the cooking. People so often repeat gender stereotypes despite people in their own experience contradicting them. That's why kids who have stay at home dads will still draw a picture of their mum cooking because that is what they think a 'mum' is.

23rd January 2011

"While a child's sex alone does not determine what is achievable, societies' (or parental) beliefs that girls and boys are innately different can limit their lives." Dr Pam Lowe, Aston University. That's such a useful quote. It was in a letter to the *Guardian* following an article about couples who pay to choose the sex of their baby. When you think about it, it's clear that wanting a particular gender of child means you already have expectations of their behaviour.

Visiting friends today, a couple of them discussed a friend's baby and how he was "such a boy" because he went from one thing to the next very quickly. He is 6 months old. It reminded me how our children's grandmother claimed that one of our nephews was "being a boy" when he messed around with his pudding, on the same day our daughter had spent all day playing with a toy garage. No one said her behaviour was "just like a girl". In fact no one noticed it. The attribution of certain behaviours to the child's gender only seems to apply when it fits the correct stereotype. Our daughter sometimes mucks around with her pudding too, but apparently this can't be attributed to her gender. Pah.

24th January 2011

Recently our daughter turned 3 and was given a marble run. She opened it with grandparents watching – her grandmother said, "I think your daddy will want to play with that too." This is an odd thing to say when she knows that marble runs are a particular favourite of Mummy in this family. But the message is made to the kid that anything mechanical is male.

Today, our daughter tells me suddenly, unprompted, about her toy baby, "My baby is a girl." I wonder why she suddenly wanted to express this. It makes me notice how important gender is to children from a young age. Picking up daughter from nursery the children crowd round the baby and ask, "Is it a boy?" I say yes and wonder, now they know this, what difference it makes to them.

25th January 2011

Only been tweeting for two weeks but have been amazed at how often there has been something to tweet about. Almost every day. An obvious one this, but a reminder of the different treatment from day one: A friend who has just had a baby girl is very popular and has a house full of cards. There is only one that isn't pink.

26th January 2011

You could write an essay on gender issues in kids TV programmes (if you have, let us know) but a couple of things to mention. Today we saw the second of two different programmes that had a plot on the embarrassment of a male

22

character because he is wearing pink. If it's OK for males to be embarrassed of being in any way 'like a girl' in quite benign kids TV shows then it's very deep in our culture.

We'll also have to do a count of male and female characters. But in a lot of the shows we watch most characters are male with one female. It's as though male characters can have different personalities but there is only one type of female.

Reading local internet forum for parents, a mum asks for advice on how to get her 3-year-old daughter to sleep. No-one knows the child personally. Advice is to bribe her, which makes sense. But with sparkly socks, or Disney Princess figures. We're currently bribing our daughter to take unpleasant medicine. The prize on offer? A wind-up torch.

When it comes to sexism there really is no business like the toy business. The Toy Awards last night included categories for boys toy and girls toy. That begs so many questions in the first place. Boys winner was a Nerf gun, girls winner the Barbie dog swimming pool. Sums it up. Violence for boys, pets and pink for girls. Hard to see how anyone 'wins' at those awards.

27th January 2011

At the doctors, a girl appears from behind us in the waiting room. Our daughter asks, "Where did she come from?" I say, "From behind you". Daughter says, "No, I mean where is her mummy?" I say, "Maybe she's here with her daddy?" Daughter is nonplussed. It's not a big surprise that she always expects a child to be with their mother, it is her usual experience of other children I suppose. Although there were actually two fathers with their children in the doctor's waiting room.

We went into the leisure centre later where they sell goggles. She cheerfully told me, "These ones are for girls and these are for boys". They were of course pink and blue goggles. I asked her if the blue ones *had* to be for boys and the pink for girls. She said no, so I asked which ones she would wear, she pointed to a purple pair.

28th January 2011

Daughter was given a small Lego alien, and it made me consider how we automatically refer to toys as 'he'. Even I couldn't stop myself when I asked, "What shall we call him? Is he a boy or a girl?" Luckily she wasn't swayed by my language though, she said, "Lucy". Unless a toy has stereotypical female features, or is a doll, people always say 'he'. Babies are usually girls though.

29th January 2011

Kids TV programme on Channel 5 just now called *Play*. It's just a mini-documentary of kids, well, playing. At first all kids play hide and seek but then just the boys are shown playing with huge water pistols which are styled on automatic machine guns.

30th January 2011

Although this diary is about how other people treat our children differently, it's making it clearer that we should look at our own behaviour. Marianne Grabrucker noticed how boys are given free rein to be unruly while girls are more compliant because they are expected to be 'good'. Boys not doing as they are told is more readily accepted because it is expected of them. Can we manage to change this in our own actions?

31st January 2011

Have had two conversations in the last 24 hours with mothers saying how their 2/3-year-old girl wants to 'mother' a smaller child or a doll. Makes me wonder if it's just the girl showing interest in a baby and that's what they label it. Boys are often interested in babies but people don't comment on it much or label it as boys wanting to 'father' the baby.

Falling asleep tonight daughter tells me how something she said, "Sounds like a boy, but I'm not, I'm a girl". I ask what a boy sounds like, she makes a sort of grunting noise as though she's lifting something heavy and says "that's like a boy". Then says in a very exaggerated high pitched voice, "but I sound like this, because I'm a girl". Which I've never heard her do before. Presumably children speak at the same pitch until puberty.

Although of course she may have noticed men and women speak at different pitches. But it seems likely that someone has been pointing out gender differences at nursery today. A boy? She fell asleep before I could ask.

3rd February 2011

Air freshener advert on TV today, daughter says the green can must be for boys, pink one for girls. This is going to be harder than I thought! And I, her dad, was wearing a pink shirt at the time!

Post-match pints with some fellow dads last night. One expresses dismay that he's found recently that he's started 'throwing like a girl'. He, like me, has one daughter and one son. I pointed out to him that language will limit his daughter's ambitions and expectations.

Talking to a father who stayed at home with his baby while his partner went back to work, he said mothers at baby groups were hostile to him. Wondering if any other male carers have found similar issues?

Our child minder was telling me earlier that (in her long experience) boys take longer to pick up things like putting on shoes and eating with cutlery. But she said she believed it's because parents and carers are more likely to do these things for boys. She said she was also guilty of this despite being aware of it. Is this due to historic cultural roles where women waited on men? Regardless of its origin it's surely a bad thing for boys to be diverted from learning to do things for themselves.

4th February 2011

The purple and grey striped jumper our baby boy is wearing under his dungarees is actually a long jumper-dress but you wouldn't know it. When I was changing him and two mothers saw that it was a dress I was surprised how shocked and disapproving they were. At 3-and-a-half months old I don't think he's all that bothered, but their reactions would give an older child a lot to think about. Girls wear trousers without any worries about their sexual identity, are boys so much more fragile? What are these mothers afraid of?

8th February 2011

A trip to the hairdresser for Mum and daughter. Every hairdresser we've ever been to has told her that she "will look like a princess". Today while discussing sitting still the hairdresser said, "You can tell Daddy when he comes home from work that Mummy sat very still". Actually Daddy was at home looking after the baby, but neither her or me told the hairdresser this, we just smiled. We should have done.

9th February 2011

Perhaps everyone following @GenderDiary should agree to contradict people when they make glib stereotypical statements. That'd be great.

11th February 2011

A couple of things today. Daughter played at a friend's house and on the way told me, "[My friend] is a *boy* who is nice you know. He doesn't hit his mummy". It was interesting that her language suggested it was unusual for a boy to be 'nice'. She's right though, of the boys we know he is definitely the most mild mannered. They had a lovely morning playing together. They played dressing up. He had a hat and said he was a doctor, she had a cape and said she was a princess. Only on Tuesday at the hairdressers was it confirmed to her that being a princess was something she should want to be. Adults have spoken to her about being a princess many more times in her life than being a doctor. I wonder what her male friend's choice of dressing up character is influenced by. I'll take note when our boy is old enough to dress up. But I'm guessing no one will have told

27

him he looks like a princess on a regular basis.

12th February 2011

What thoughts do you all have about not buying children toys in stereotypical colours/styles? Our daughter wanted a bike for Christmas and we looked hard for a gender neutral one but she requested it have handlebar streamers and a baby seat on the back. Obviously only the 'girl' bikes had these accessories. We did get her one. It's hard to withhold things when she is too young to understand your ideology. Seeing the gendered bikes in the park today makes me wish we hadn't. Have any of you done it?

Should we state whether it's dad or mum tweeting? Or is that defeating the purpose somewhat? I mean should we specify who is authoring each tweet? I'm inclined not to.

Some classic stuff from a dads and kids meet-up this afternoon. 4-year-old girl showing off ballet moves she learnt at class this morning. 2-year-old brother copies by lifting leg up and a dad says, "Oh he's like Jean Claude Van Damme". Wow.

Two girls there go off to play with a dolls house and a dad points to this as 'typical' of girls, evidence of innate differences. Girls return and start playing with toy tool kit, one drilling one hammering a door. Same dad barely registers that 'untypical' behaviour. The doll's house was upstairs everyone else is downstairs. Are the girls' actions indicative of confidence to play away from parents/adults? Plus my girl only knew of the doll's house because when we arrived the 3-year-old boy of the host took her off to play with it. No-one commented until the two girls were playing with the doll's house.

Our 4-year-old girl was a bit shy and clingy when first arrived. It was blamed on the fact all the toys of the 3-year-old host are 'boys toys'. But it didn't faze our daughter. She was happily playing with trucks, fire engines etc and no-one comments. Yet if what is said about 'boys toys' is true then her behaviour is unusual and therefore surely more worthy of comment? Gender attitudes are self-reinforcing.

16th February 2011

Some thought provoking stuff this week that is not black and white. Marianne Grabrucker wrote about boys dominating play so girls had to adapt their behaviour. Yesterday our daughter played with a boy who is the stereotype of a 'boy's boy'. As with every time they play he wants whatever the other child has, not to play with it though, but in order to have ownership of it and to be the one in charge. I've seen girls be possessive of toys too though, and they will also take something just to have ownership. But it never escalates to the same level as with this boy. We end up taking the toy away from them both, so the girl loses out even though she has done nothing. Grabrucker argues that the girl has to adapt to the boy's behaviour which sets them up for the patriarchal world. I think children of both genders would behave like this if they could. I can only conclude boys do it more because they are allowed to do so.

19th February 2011

A 3-year-old's birthday party today and there were a lot of

things we could tweet about, but one thing struck me (mum) most; daughter had mentioned wearing a dress to the party but had forgotten by the time we left so I didn't remind her. When we arrived the birthday girl and a friend were in party dresses. I immediately worried that my girl would feel left out, but this was my worry not hers. I remembered a birthday party I had been to as a child where I didn't know most of the children and they had bullied me because I wore boyish clothes. I suppose this experience pushed me into conforming more in what I wore. I wanted to fit in. Will she? For the record the boys were wearing their everyday clothes just like my daughter. When she was a bridesmaid she learned, and said, people "like me" in a pretty dress. She noticed they give her special attention for it. I'd rather she got a compliment for something she did or said, but I expect she'll remember to put on a dress next time. I won't stop her if she wants to.

24th February 2011

At a playground today daughter played with a boy who was dressed in beige and brown and was very forthright. If they were on a boat he said, "I'm the captain" or if I tried to help he said, "I can do that" repeatedly. When he left daughter said, "There she goes". I asked why she thought he was a girl. She said, "She's got long hair". Interesting that for a 3-year-old long hair was the most important way to define gender despite other signifiers. He had a ponytail. Though I suppose actually I don't know for sure whether she/he was a boy or a girl.

4th March 2011

It's been a very gender-quiet week. How nice.

6th March 2011

So I should start by saying that the National Railway Museum is really great and we had a great time there, however the museum had a kids' science presentation about Newton's Laws – the way forces make trains move. The show needed audience volunteers. Every single child called up as a volunteer was a boy until they did an experiment with a Barbie doll. The presenter asked if there were any Barbie fans who wanted to help. A whole pack of cubs had their hands in the air but finally a girl volunteer was picked. Poor Barbie got fired out of a cannon and her legs broke off, much to the amusement of the audience. An earlier experiment used two toy elephants to demonstrate how weight affects force, one was in pink and one in blue. The blue elephant had eaten a full English breakfast and was heavy. The pink elephant had had a glass of water and was on a diet. Science is so often gender segregated and this was no exception.

9th March 2011

Thanks to @rhiannongwyn and others who have suggested we write a blog. We can't find the time to do it properly at the moment, we hope tweets will do.

11th March 2011

Yesterday a friend came to play with her 3-year-old boy and

1-year-old girl. I asked what toys they would like me to get out. I suggested Duplo, musical instruments, cars or dressing up. My friend said she was sure her boy would want to play with the cars. He didn't seem more interested in them than any other toys to me. Later she asked her girl, "Wouldn't you like to try on the fairy wings?" She said no. I often see blatant directing of children into gendered play like this, yet parents don't notice their own influence. Isn't it obvious?!

15th March 2011

A friend said her 3-year-old boy asked her "What do you call a girl's willie?" and she didn't know what to say. She asked me what we call it. I said when our daughter was a baby we called her genitals her 'fandango' but didn't often say that any more. We agreed it was a shame that names for girls' genitals are so overlooked. Marianne Grabrucker gave her daughter's genitals the name Mary-Ann and used the name frequently. Boys genitals are obviously more prominent and are easily talked about, but why should it be that we don't talk about girls' genitals?

19th March 2011

What I've noticed most of all by keeping this diary is the acceptance of raising boys to shun anything with female connotations. So where girls wear clothes, or read books, or watch films about both genders, the same is not true of boys. And we accept this. There has to be a point where we ask what messages it sends to boys to be brought up to always reject the female realm.

20th March 2011

Talking to a friend whose son is 4 in a few weeks. She's talking about the difficulty of making him the dinosaur birthday cake he wants. No such problems with her 7-month-old daughter, she's already got a fairy princess castle recipe lined up.

25th March 2011

The @GenderDiary family is at Peppa Pig World (sigh). I am pleased to say it is measuring up very well so far in the gender-neutral stakes. But even though the main character is Peppa, all the 'boys' clothes have her brother George on. Boys can't be seen wearing the female character.

27th March 2011

On train to the TUC march yesterday a granny was telling another woman that her granddaughter is excited about a new baby. Granny said, "If it's a boy you can play football with him." The friend interjects to say she could play football with a girl, "It could turn out to be a tomboy." Close. Actually she could play football with a girl because girls can like football on their own terms!

29th March 2011

In M&S Bromley this afternoon with the two kids. Shop assistant says to me "You babysitting this afternoon?" I said nothing. I should've said "NO I'm just a man in a shop with his two children!" Where does one begin??

30th March 2011

Visiting a friend at the weekend who has a 1-year-old son. He's walking. She reminds me "boys mobilise, girls socialise". This is a mantra I've often shared, I think it's true to some extent, BUT not because of inherent differences, it's because sexes are treated differently from birth. She says she can only speak from experience with her son, that's her scientific experiment. I point out that's not science. If it was how science works I'd look at my children and conclude all boys have blue eyes, all girls have brown eyes! Today's @GenderDiary lesson must surely be to tell people at every opportunity to see the difference between anecdote and evidence.

2nd April 2011

Daughter is at an age when we're thinking about first trip to cinema. Easter releases for kids seem to be *Rio*, *Hop* or *Turtle Story*. All got male lead characters. Not a problem but I say we should have a rule that every second film we see with kids must have a female lead. Trouble is will we ever go to the cinema again?! Anyone know of forthcoming films with female leads?

6th April 2011

Get ready for a gender tweetathon. Got lots saved up. Hopefully the baby will stay asleep.

First up, an anecdote about a 6-year-old who has always been indulged in the fetishism of pink/princesses/Barbies. She has black hair but whenever she draws a picture of herself she draws blonde hair and blue eyes. When asked why, she says that that's what she wants to look like and doesn't want to look like herself. Gulp.

On the way to a pre-school fair this weekend our daughter asked if there would be face painting and could she be a pirate? On the way in we pass two girls with pink butterflies on their faces. Several people in our party tell them how nice they look. We sit down to get her face painted and the painter asks, "What do you want and what's your favourite colour?" I was gobsmacked, she asked for a pink butterfly. She had only told me earlier her favourite colour was red. The face painter whispered to me she was bored of pink and was running out.

Another anecdote about a 2-year-old who is a regular mountain goat, always climbing everything. She was climbing the gate outside her pre-school as she does every day. Her grandparent tried to take her down thinking it unsafe. She protests and the grandparent says, "Fine, you be a tomboy." The words were not meant as a criticism but the implication is that a typical girl child wouldn't climb or be interested in it.

My daughter and her cousins were playing dressing-up, she had put on fairy wings but was bored of them and asked for something else. We offered her a devil, a witch and a police helmet. She says, "No! I want something PRETTY!" This feminist tried not to look horrified! Don't be too harsh on me for that last comment, Twitter!

Thanks for all the lovely mentions for us today. We're so glad you find it interesting. Just to say, not many mentions for our baby boy at the moment, although I notice people tell me how strong/big he is more often than I remember with my daughter. Possibly I just notice it more, or possibly people say it more often. (Possibly he's bigger and stronger...)

How could I forget this one: I'm talking with my nephew about something that is broken, he says, "You need your daddy to fix it for you". I ask why, he says because his daddy fixes things. I ask if mummy could fix things. "No, only daddies fix things". I ask why he thinks that. He says, "Because I've never seen Mummy fix anything". I remind him how I (his aunt) fixed his DVD player.

7th April 2011

Talking to another dad after football about primary schools. His son starts in September, our daughter will start next year. He says he's not concerned about which school his baby daughter will go to because girls have a different way of learning. His son however needs more structure because he's a boy. His daughter is six months, how can he know what sort of education will suit her? Both children being brought up in the same house by the same parents, yet he's convinced gender will determine how they learn from day one at school.

8th April 2011

The @GenderDiary family are off to Germany, home of Marianne Grabrucker, for a week. We'll report back on what's changed in the last 30 years.

18th April 2011

Most interesting thing happened on Sunday. Both of us were looking for books to read at bedtime with our daughter. She found a bookmark with a cartoon of a girl with bunches on it. She said it was for her, but it couldn't be for Daddy. We asked why. She said it could be for Mummy because it was a girl. When pressed she explained that because it looked like her then it was '*for*' her. It seemed clear how clearly she sees representations of girls as meaning something is '*for*' her, or that she belongs in that sphere. Have got many more things to tweet. Will try to do it later this evening.

So, here's a list of things the children's grandmother told me were due to being a boy this week: concentrating very hard on the TV, having a large appetite as a baby, not doing things for themselves like getting dressed. Describes my daughter to a tee.

The kids' cousin had an interesting thing to say when @GenderDiary dad was taking out his contact lenses. He said contact lenses were only for girls. In his experience only his mother wears contact lenses and he had obviously put this down to her gender. He is 6 and it's interesting how early kids will attribute arbitrary things to gender rather than another factor like having blue eyes or being a doctor, both of which are attributes of his mother. We told him men wore contacts too but he didn't seem very convinced.

Will tweet the rest tomorrow. By the way, we're both reading *Delusions of Gender* by Cordelia Fine. Get yourselves a copy as soon as you can.

20th April 2011

Here's a marvellous quote for you from Cordelia Fine's *Delusions of Gender*, "Cultural realities and beliefs about females and males represented in existing inequalities; in commercials; in conversations; in the minds, expectations or behaviour of others; or primed in our own minds by the environment – alter our self-perception, interests and behaviour."

Ditto this quote by sociologists Celia Ridgeway and Shelley Correll, "Cultural beliefs about gender act like a weight on the scale that modestly but systematically differentiates the behaviour and evaluations of otherwise similar men and women."

We were away last week with relatives who have a 6-year-old boy and a 4-year-old girl. While I was sat breastfeeding, the girl came over to me asked what I was doing and then we chatted about various things. Both her mother and father separately asked me if she had come to talk to me about babies because she was so into them. I told them it didn't seem that way to me. Meanwhile her brother had requested to hold and cuddle the baby on three or four occasions and for quite some time. His sister never did this. No one commented on his interest at all.

Incidentally at the airport in Munich two separate boys around the age of two or three took particular interest in our baby and were encouraged to do so by their parents, which was nice to see.

24th April 2011

Our 3-year-old is totally unaware of the Royal Wedding at the moment. What are you all planning to do with your kids on *that* day?

27th April 2011

The kids' grandmother was telling me how she had been trying to get her son-in-law to fix her grandson's bike tyre so they could go out. I asked why her or my sister thought they couldn't do it. She looked flummoxed and agreed they probably could.

Being able to speak very little German meant we didn't have many lengthy chats about gender while we were away. But I noticed something interesting on the plane. A flight attendant asked "How old is she?" referring to our boy who was wearing gender neutral clothes. It occurred to me that they would have similar conversations very frequently and be well versed in not saying the wrong thing. I wondered if they think that a parent with a girl baby would be more offended at the child being called a boy than vice versa.

Saw our childminder who will be looking after our baby boy later in the year. She was tipping him upside down and saying, "Ah yes you like things a bit rough. Yes, boys do." She did then temper it by saying that his sister was like that too. But I think physical treatment of boys is subtly different in so many ways.

I've really been noticing how female leads in children's books – fairy tales most often, but other genres too – are referred to as beautiful. This is often the only description of them and is always seen as a virtue and something relevant. Even female characters that are animals are described this way. So Perdita in *101 Dalmations* is introduced as a beautiful dog. I often leave out these words when reading.

Would be good to see the methodology for this research from the Geena Davis Research Institute – "They found that the more hours of television a girl watches, the fewer options she believes she has in life, and the more hours a boy watches, the more sexist his views become." (*Life Imitates Art: Geena Davis on how gender inequality on TV and in movies has a powerful impact on kids*, The Wall Street Journal, 11th April 2011). Yikes.

28th April 2011

Delusions of Gender by Cordelia Fine really is bloody fantastic. @GenderDiary would like to buy the whole world a copy. The piece I was just reading that explains how girls' ability in maths depends on which country they are from is fascinating. 'Innate' and 'hardwired' are such overused and misunderstood words.

29th April 2011

Following on from last night's maths tweet. The only thing I've heard Kate Middleton say recently while doing a meet and greet with students:

Kate: What are you studying?

Student: Maths.

Kate: Oh gosh, really?!

Jessica Smith's review of *Delusions of Gender* for the F-Word makes reference to something I've been trying to do recently. Refer to 'children' rather than 'boys and girls'.

Bank holidays + family = Gender Diary material. More on this later.

I came in at the end of a conversation between grandparent and my daughter. Grandmother: "You need your daddy to build the train," referring to some Duplo. I say, "Why does she need daddy?!" Grandmother claims that he had made the train really quickly once before and then protested that she is told off by me too often. But honestly, how hard is it to build a train with Duplo?! It's insulting to three generations of females in the room to suggest we need a man, who's not here (he's working), to stick toy bricks together for us.

Later we went for a walk in the woods with my sister, brother-in-law and three children. It reminded me of an entry in Marianne Grabrucker's diary where she describes little girls pushing toy prams being unable to run and play freely while so tied down. I noticed how myself and my sister were pushing buggies while the kids and my brother-in-law mucked about and he showed them interesting things. I consciously tried to leave the buggy sometimes and get involved because otherwise I felt like we were behaving just like in Marianne's diary from over 30 years ago.

1st May 2011

A Cordelia Fine quote on pink and blue for you, "So thoroughly have these preferences become ingrained that psychologists and journalists now speculate on the genetic and evolutionary origins of gendered colour preferences that are little more than fifty years old."

2ⁿᵈ May 2011

I saw a t-shirt in Mothercare with the slogan 'Daddy's Girl', but I'm guessing they don't make the equivalent 'Mummy's Boy' t-shirt for boys.

Interestingly there are lots more colours for boys clothes in the shops. Purple, pink and yellow are new and very welcome, however they often come with a signifier to remind us this is a boy.

3ʳᵈ May 2011

Another example of how gender seems so important that kids attach a relevance to it that doesn't exist. Daughter said, "Mummies don't go to the hairdressers with children. Only daddies go with children and mummies stay at home to look after the baby." Oddly her mum has taken her the last two times, but before that it was usually dad.

We've tweeted before about how kids assume something is only for one gender because in their house someone takes that role. But I think it highlights the way kids use gender as the thing to differentiate rather than, say, blue eyes. Our language and behaviours attach importance to the difference between male and female, so kids do as well.

4ᵗʰ May 2011

Incidentally, a way that we've treated the kids differently is that our boy has had books like *I Love Kittens* from the library which we wouldn't have picked for our girl. It's to try to counter-balance all the gender stereotypical stuff they'll get outside the home so it's justified. Gender-neutral parenting is, of course, an impossibility.

Also, I tried to change one of the animals in a Dr Seuss book to 'she' last night. Our daughter corrected me. I asked why it wasn't a she, she said she just knew it wasn't. To be fair she's read it quite a few times before. There are very few female characters in Dr Seuss.

6th May 2011

An update on what is turning out to be kid's fashion week on @GenderDiary. My 9-year-old nephew just triumphantly told me about his new trainers. "What colour do you think my laces are?" he asked. I said I had no idea. "Pink!" he beamed. So pink *is* in fashion for boys. I should mention that this nephew has rarely been seen in anything other than navy blue and sludge-brown before. Laces are a good start.

Meanwhile our 3-year-old isn't down with the nuances of fashion. She told me earlier, "Remember how I said blue swimming goggles are for boys and pink for girls? Well that's because girls are pink and boys are blue." I asked what she meant literally, saying, "but you're not pink". She looked down at her clothes and repeated it. I asked if she meant clothes and she said yes. I said that boys don't *have* to wear blue and girls pink. She insisted they do (even though she was wearing blue). I insisted they didn't, she said they did. Etc etc.

9th May 2011

We were about to go out in the children's grandmother's car this weekend when she realised her tyre was low. She explained this to our daughter saying, "We'll have to go in daddy's... (Pause for thought).... AND mummy's car." If you persist it seems others change their thinking too.

Dentist visit for the family today. They usually give stickers to reward kids. Disney Princess ones were promised and @GenderDiary Dad pointed out that we wouldn't be that thrilled about it. The female dentist told us her male nurse only got those ones out for girls and had Rupert Bear ones for boys. The dentist said even if he offers both he holds the gender-specific one further forward. Our daughter was eventually given one of each. Again, we hope our comments might have made them think about their assumptions.

While turning on the TV for our daughter the previous channel comes up. It's the news channel playing a story about Osama Bin Laden. She says, "I don't like mens (sic!), I like ladies." I ask what she means and she just repeats it even when I remind her that Daddy is a man. She briefly says she doesn't like men's voices but then reverts to saying she doesn't like 'mens'. It makes me feel a bit sad.

12th May 2011

Stuck in watching TV with a kid covered in chicken pox. Feeling furious at the lack of female characters we're seeing and about their names: Petal, Precious, Sweetie etc. It's as though the television is trying to wind me up. #angermanagementFAIL

13th May 2011

It's not surprising kids think all gender neutral animals are male. Show me an adult who doesn't use 'he' as a default and I'd be shocked.

16th May 2011

A lesson learnt about calling things by their correct name: As we mentioned once about naming genitals, we've been known to call a vagina a fandango. Who would have thought that word would ever appear in a different context in a kids TV programme. But today a puppet vegetable fennel was doing the tango and they called it 'the fandango'. Cue hilarious confusion. We should have just used the word vagina.

20th May 2011

A visit to the Natural History Museum inevitably ends in the gift shop. They have a toy pack that contains a diver and plastic sea animals, and a pack with plastic bones and a dinosaur hunter. Both diver and dinosaur hunter are male. Why? It's even more nutty when on other side of the shop wall is an exhibit about Mary Anning, described as the 'greatest fossil hunter ever known' by the Natural History Museum.

Daughter yesterday says, "When I grow up I'm going to be a princess AND a pirate". Is it a sign we're succeeding in balance? Or failing because we can't stop the all pervasive princess culture?

24th May 2011

A trip to second rate animal park Eagle Heights at the weekend and there was lots of Cub Scout groups there. The cubs were all boys, the leaders all middle-aged/elderly women. What are the implications for boys' role models? When I was a cub, leaders were a range of ages and gender. Are men now afraid of nonce jokes? And boys get the message that volunteering-leadership is for women? Will they then ask why leaders in national life are not women?

25th May 2011

Just remembered a conversation with a colleague the other day. Small talk included him telling me how his teenage boys don't want to wear high visibility jackets when cycling because, "They'll look like girls". It's a well accepted insult isn't it? #bah.

26th May 2011

On the swings with the kids and two girls about 14 are swinging next to us. A girl of about 9 starts climbing the metal frame of the swing and, because she's wearing her school skirt, we all see her pants as she crouches on the bar. One of the girls says, "That's a bit expla..expli... what's it called?" They eventually agree the word they are looking for is "explicit". They laugh like drains for quite a while. The 9-year-old leaves quickly. Our daughter watches all this with wide eyed interest but says nothing.

27th May 2011

We were interviewed by Emily Craig (@emilyjoanhc) this week for a radio documentary she's making about gender and education. Sure it will be marvellous! The documentary considers the Swedish approach to gender in pre-school.

28th May 2011

We love them dearly but the kids' grandparents provide valuable fodder for this diary. Arriving after they are in bed their grandmother sees the newly acquired Playmobil castle/fort our daughter has been given. She says "A fort? I won't know how to play with her with that." "Why?" I ask. "I just wouldn't know what to do. It makes me think of fighting." I say it's just like other imaginary play – a building with people in it. A doll's house for example.

1st June 2011

Yikes. We've just been followed by @BabyGenderPlan "Plan Your Baby's Gender". Not planning to click on that link. May just be spam?

Forgive me if I'm wrong but it's legal in parts of the USA, no? I'll go and google it. By which I mean being able to choose the sex. There was a piece in the Guardian (*Sex Selection: Getting the Baby you want*, The Guardian 3rd April 2010) last year about people in this country travelling abroad so they could choose.

There was a great letter in the paper the following week which we still have stuck on our wall. I've quoted it before but will again. (*See 26th June*)

7th June 2011

Here's an interesting one. A friend's cat gets stuck in a neighbour's shed while they are on holiday. I'm busy talking about the cat on the phone. That cat's name is Sugar and he's male. Our daughter says, "That's a girl's name". I ask her to explain why she thinks that is associated with the female and therefore not appropriate for the male. I assume this but she couldn't explain herself enough to be sure.

Sorry we've been a bit quiet. Having had chicken pox in the house we've been mixing with the world less, therefore having less material. And thanks to all the new people who have chosen to follow. Please feel free to send us any of your experiences so we can retweet them.

9th June 2011

I was at parliament this week for Jean Kilbourne speaking to an all-party group on body image, organised by Jo Swinson MP. Jean Kilbourne was a pioneer on how adverts affect body image, she invented the discipline. And she is really nice. Look up her film *Killing Us Softly* on YouTube. Brilliant, funny and incisive. But I think Jean Kilbourne missed a trick in considering not just kids' ads more fully but the extent that kids are gendered before they even see their first ad. Girlguiding offered an interesting point. Girls' role models are Katie Price/Perry etc, but the values they want are courage and to triumph over adversity.

12th June 2011

Went for coffee with a friend, his son (4) and my daughter.

The kids have cookies and crumbs are everywhere, but he only comments on his lad as a 'typical boy'.

15th June 2011

I find the 'pink' thing is like a creeping contagion. On Monday our daughter wanted to choose her clothes for nursery, "I want pink leggings because Hannah at nursery's favourite colour is pink."

Then at a friend's house playing with a girl and a boy of a similar age. The other children fight over who gets a pink cup and plate for their tea. Our daughter then says she wants pink too. Which never happens at home.

23rd June 2011

We've been in a holiday internet black hole for a while. Thanks for your tweets. Will retweet them later.

25th June 2011

The pink creep continues for our daughter. She was choosing a temporary tattoo from a sheet. They were all butterflies in different colours. She said, "I want the pink one, because it's the pretty one." The butterflies are all the same shape so it must be colour that signifies prettiness to her. So the colour alone is now shorthand for it. Pink is no longer just a colour, it is loaded with meaning.

26th June 2011

I said I'd post the ace reply to the article on baby sex

selection from the Guardian letters page ages ago. (*1ˢᵗ June*)
Coming next:

"*Your article on sex selection matches my own studies in the area to some extent. However, you overlooked the most important element. People want to choose a child's sex because they believe that sex will determine certain gendered qualities within an imagined child. This can range from boys carrying on the family line to the fetishism of pink princesses in girls. Having set this course for an unborn child, this influences families' understanding and potential treatment of the child, impacting on the child's life chances. While a child's sex alone does not determine what is achievable, societies' (or parental) beliefs that boys and girls are innately different can limit their lives.*" Dr Pam Lowe, Senior lecturer in sociology, Aston University.

How great is that? It's stuck up in our toilet so most people who visit our house read it. Sneaky, eh? She sums up what we feel very well.

27ᵗʰ June 2011

So, our daughter's favourite film is the old Disney animation *Robin Hood*. When learning this, at least three people have mentioned that she'd make a great Maid Marion or something similar about Maid Marion. She has always identified with Robin Hood – but people want to apply a rule that she must identify with a character of the same gender. It's the same issue we've seen before about gender being taken note of and considered more important than any other aspect of a person's character.

One about the baby as well today. The old classic, "He's such a boy!" The comment came just from looking at him, he wasn't doing anything. I was holding him. Someone else asked, "How old is she?" about five minutes later.

28th June 2011

At a magic show. The magician asks the kids in the audience their names. One girl is shy, so he says, "Girls are often a bit more embarrassed." He ignores my daughter desperately trying to get his attention so she'll be asked! Later in the show our daughter gets to go on stage to help with a trick. A little boy also goes up. The magician banters with them, only my daughter is asked, "Are you married?" Mum and Dad aren't married never mind the 3-year-old daughter. When the little boy is asked he says he wants to be a shopkeeper when he grows up. My girl says she wants to be a pirate.

29th June 2011

Been thinking about this Lisa Bloom piece *How to talk to little girls* (Huffington Post, 22nd June 2011), without the words 'Hello, what a pretty DRESS!' and knowing we also need to learn how to talk to boys. Research shows we talk to them much less.

8th July 2011

Things that are due to being a boy No.1743: Being hot. Grandparent: "I think that's a boy thing because [name of other boy] is always hot."

9th July 2011

Bought a fleece for son. It's mainly blue with pink stripes but was in the girls section. Who decides how much pink makes an item female?

Also the first time he wore it was the first time in eight months he's been mistaken for a girl.

To the cinema last week with some trepidation for *Tinkerbell and the Great Fairy Rescue*. Part of my rule that every second film we see has a female lead. The worry is that even female led films will feature nothing but princesses, fairies etc. Tinkerbell was OK though.

10th July 2011

Heh. I see @GenderDiary Dad tweeted that no one had mistaken the baby for a girl recently, when I tweeted that it happened a few weeks ago.

11th July 2011

Tonight our daughter was cutting up an old card with pictures of cakes on it, "The beautiful cakes are the girls' cakes, and the not good ones are boys." I say boys are beautiful too. She says no. I tell her that means she's saying her dad and brother aren't beautiful. She says that's right. Today is a nursery day. Things like this often get said after being at nursery.

13th July 2011

Just remembered a they're-like-that-because-they're-a-boy/girl thing from the weekend. A mum tells me her baby girl "is feisty because she's a girl". Although it's nice to hear a more unusual generalisation about girls (instead of them being 'good' compared to boys), it is nonetheless something being applied as being caused by gender, when it's really just down to personality.

14th July 2011

Something I've noticed recently is how many women put themselves down in front of their kids. It's not surprising they do it with the pressures that advertising and the media place on women and their appearance. But you can see how children will listen and be affected.

Please tell me the new Smurf film doesn't have only one female Smurf. Please no.

16th July 2011

Went to a primary school fair today. The 'Test your strength' stall had prizes of toy guns, swords and bows & arrows. There were boys everywhere with weapons. One was heard to say, "Anyone who doesn't want to be friends gets shot!" I didn't see any girls with the prizes.

22nd July 2011

Spent afternoon at daughter's nursery 'graduation' for those leaving to go to school. Entertainment included balloon animals and face painting. Face painting was a very strict gender split of pink butterflies or cats for girls and tigers for boys. Reactions from adults for girls, "Don't you look pretty/beautiful". For boys, less comment, but usually, "Don't you look scary." Kids were aged 3-4 and were asked by the painter what they wanted. Shows how fixed gender conformity is by this age. Daughter chose a tiger when she was 2 but since being 3 has always asked for a pink butterfly. The painter asks each child their favourite colour too. She says pink, although doesn't say this at home.

25th July 2011

Today I've been noticing in my own thoughts how strong the impulse is to look at my baby boy's behaviour and compare it to his sister's; how I could think, while reading a book with him for example, "He's a boy, he'd rather be active", even though his sister may have acted in a similar way. But would some people then make less of an effort to continue with the book with a boy? This would allow boys more opportunity to be active and girls to be more static, bookish and to be talked to. Does this allow boys more 'freedom', but at the expense of communication skills?

28th July 2011

Just saw a poster for the Smurf movie. I was gobsmacked. Yes, in 2011 there is still just one female. Because being female is a character trait y'know. Going to have to look up the plot of the current Smurf film now. Ug.

Smurf plot: They are in New York and have to get home. Jeez, no one has EVER thought of that idea before. I'm so sorry I had to share that. No mention of the ratio of male to female Smurfs in the coming film. Posters suggest it's one Smurfette. Could @thefworduk do an #audit?!

Incidentally I see Studio Ghibli's new film of the Borrowers is out soon, with title changed to the name of the female lead Arrietty. Good.

29th July 2011

Daughter settled no bother at all when she first went to the childminder. Fair to say our son is less keen, but still only his first week. I was telling someone that it had been a little difficult and she says, "Well he's a boy." What does that even mean?? #blamegenderforeverything

30th July 2011

Daughter is talking in the park. She says to me, "There's a mummy squirrel. The daddy squirrel is out at work." I say, "That squirrel is looking for food, that's squirrel work! Just like your mummy goes to work."

Maternity leave only being economically viable for the woman in our house has given our daughter access to a classic standard view of men going to work while women stay at home. Maternity leave is over now, so it will be interesting to see how fixed her assumptions are.

6th August 2011

Earlier I caught myself thinking, "When our daughter's friend comes to play he'll really enjoy playing with her Playmobil castle." I then remembered in our last two visits to his house his mother had got out a Fisher Price doll's house specifically for our daughter. I disregarded it at the time as me just being very 'gender-sensitive', after all, it's a toy belonging to a boy. But now I see she probably had the same train of thought as me, which is basically directing children to toys based on their gender. I'll ask her next time.

7th August 2011

We've been watching #Cbeebies for 45mins and only heard one female character speak. Do me a favour world.

12th August 2011

Today our daughter says: "Girls wear bows in their hair. Boys can't. If a boy wore a bow I'd tell him I wouldn't be his friend any more." Cue long conversation about all the problems with those statements. It's amazing what has been picked up by the age of 3-and-a-half.

15th August 2011

A wedding this weekend. Interesting for kids to hear in the speeches the many references to the bride's appearance but never to the groom's. To be fair to them, they walked into the church together and both made speeches. Quite modern!

Books come up frequently in the diary gender divide. I saw Anne Frank's *The Diary of a Young Girl* in the library today with a sticker on that says 'Something for the girls'. The sticker may as well say: 'BOYS! Despite the lessons for all of humankind in this book, it is about a GIRL and therefore not for you!'

17th August 2011

Amazing. Just heard a UK survey shows, on average, boys

get 32p more pocket money than girls. We start the gender pay gap in the home! Awful. We keep this diary purely to record the way kids experience the world differently because of their gender, because so many people believe they don't.

19th August 2011

Diet book aimed at 6-12year old girls! (*A diet book for six-year-old girls: the worst idea ever?* The Guardian, 17th August 2011)

22nd August 2011

I am dressing our baby boy and putting him in his pink polo shirt (sold as a boy's shirt). Discussion with 6-year-old nephew as follows:

6-year-old: Why are you doing that?

Me: I'm getting him dressed

6-year-old: But why are you dressing him in that?

Me: These are his clothes

6-year-old: But it's pink

Me: Yes, it's a colour. I'm wearing red. What colour are you wearing?

6-year-old: Blue, I always wear blue.

End

On a long train journey, got a Bob the Builder magazine for our daughter. On the magazine's letters page Bob is saying "JOIN MY TEAM!" above photos of young readers. Apparently only boys are in his 'team'.

1st September 2011

Spy Kids film adverts. Just in case you weren't completely aware that she's a girl and he's a boy. Pink/blue spy 'aura'.

3rd September 2011

Nephew (4) is very keen on wearing button-up shirts. When his mum asks why he says: "Because they're pretty. Boys can't wear dresses, so when I wear my shirt I can look pretty like [my sister] when she wears a dress." He enjoys going to choose his clothes in the mornings.

Another one of these. My niece was having a 'Pirates and Mermaids' week at pre-school. She was a pirate and a member of staff told her mum when she came to pick her up, "She's too beautiful to be a pirate, why isn't she a mermaid?" Even at age 2, appearance is the message.

We get a lot of @GenderDiary material from the kids' cousins. Oldest nephew (of a set of siblings) is off to school in a few weeks. Will be interesting to see how long his favourite colour remains pink and his favourite dressing up costume remains a fairy.

4th September 2011

That post reminds me we need to share some positive stuff here as well as moaning about the bad stuff. Our discussions about language, not using 'he' as default, and seeking out more gender-balanced books has been good. Also challenging those people who enforce stereotypes on our kids and trying to make them recognise the things they say are what shape our children's identities. The thing I've learnt most from this diary is that our own gender prejudices run deep, however aware we think we are.

6th September 2011

A friend tells me her daughter had been playing with two male friends, she overheard one say, "This is a boys game so you can't play." They are aged 3. Shows a very firm understanding of the differences between them at age 3 and understanding that there is gender appropriate behaviour.

I've been thinking about more ways to be a positive feminist parent. Can people share some suggestions here for pre-school books that include characters that REALLY depart from gender stereotypes, also are there any books with LGBT characters, particularly parents?

MT @BurlyQEinstein: *The Shy Creatures* by David Mack is brilliant

RT @RosamundUrwin: *The Paperbag Princess*

RT @RevDebra: Books for small children with LG parents: *Heather has Two Mommies* and *Daddy's Roomate* were favorites of mine when mine were little. Also *My Princess Boy* and *Free to Be… You and Me* is a classic with some great stories.

13th September 2011

Jeremy Vine's BBC Radio 2 show has got us into deep discussion (I know, I know). Anyone got a link to the news story about the kid with gender dysphoria?

Here it is: *Mother of transgender girl says adults, not children, taunt her* (Pink News, 12th September 2011).

19th September 2011

The @GenderDiary family are very busy with us both back at work now. Good job we didn't start a blog, can hardly find time to tweet. But here's some stuff from the weekend.

A 3rd birthday party with a kids' entertainer. Prizes and treats for musical bumps as follows: stickers and balloon dogs for girls, bouncy balls and balloon swords for boys. Our daughter was the only girl to be given a sword. Later I saw another girl had got hold of one and was playing with the boys. I'm not a fan of weapons but boys are clearly expected to be.

27th September 2011

Out with dads last night, two of whom have kids just starting school. One a daughter, one a son. Both are asked how the kids are settling in. No more questions to the dad with a daughter but the one with a son is asked if the boy has a girlfriend yet, does he fancy his teacher etc. Interesting that even for a 4-year-old, school is apparently about sex as much as education. Then we wonder why girls get better results.

29th September 2011

Anyone got thoughts on whether it's right or wrong to point out the gender biases people have in raising their kids? My point of view (influenced by Cordelia Fine) is that small suggestions can alter people's ways of thinking in subtle ways. But done with respect.

RT @leahmouse: In theory yes, but I don't think you'd have many friends left if you did it frequently. Maybe just model the alternative.

RT @Bex6810: No... surely it's their business how to bring up their own children? Why should anyone have the right to judge.

30th September 2011

Overheard at One o'clock Club - A mum: "Yes, she'll be in dungarees with just a t-shirt or something with a bit of pink. It's ok for girls to wear whatever. But you can't do it with boys. My mum bought him some jeans without realising they were girl's ones with pink stitching well I just couldn't do that to him."

5th October 2011

It's Gender Segregated Christmas Catalogue time again[1]. Boots do this EVERY year. Get a grip Boots. I don't think Boots the Chemist tweet, but if anyone knows any different please let me know.

6th October 2011

From my sister today: Using a float on each arm yesterday was called a 'butterfly' in her daughter's all girl swimming class. Today in her son's all boy class they are called aeroplanes. Gah!

9th October 2011

Kudos to the Early Learning Centre. In their Xmas catalogue, kids of both genders playing with all toys. Not perfect but better than most. When all kids toy catalogues have a boy wearing a pink princess dressing-up outfit, then we'll be getting somewhere!

24th October 2011

The @GenderDiary family life is so hectic sometimes it's hard to find time to tweet. The baby has had his first birthday now and is walking.

News from my niece's all girl swimming lessons – The teacher: "You can play with the balls now. What colour would you like? You don't have to tell me. I already know it's pink". Gah.

And at lunch yesterday, a friend's daughter says purple is her favourite colour. Her dad says, "Purple isn't your favourite colour. It's pink of course." And last week in the library our daughter was colouring with some school girls. The oldest was boasting that she had a picture of a princess and a pink crayon and none of the others did. The reaction from all of them was, "I'm going to colour mine pink too." Reinforcement of pink culture happens to girls on a daily basis.

27th October 2011

Today it occurs to me that girls must live with a constant low-level hum of concern about what people think of them in a way that boys don't.

1st November 2011

Just seen a Lego advert on Channel 4. It's about fathers and sons building together. I look forward to the one about mothers and daughters building together, because that is a regular occurrence in our house. Don't let me down Lego. Remember your advert *What it is beautiful* from 1981.

Hello @LEGO_Group Just seen a UK advert about dads and sons building together. That's really nice. Is there one for mums and daughters too?

2nd November 2011

Shame we haven't had a reply from the @LEGO_Group as I'm a genuine fan of it as a toy for all. If any of you had a reply do let us know.

4th November 2011

Our daughter's friend came round to play today.

Her: Let's play dressing up.

Him: Are they boys' or girls' dressing up clothes?

Her: Um, girls'?

Me: They're for children. Anyone can wear whatever they want.

She chose to be a bee. He was a skeleton and a dragon.

6th November 2011

We had an @GenderDiary-family moment yesterday that

made my blood boil and we were all there to witness it. We were browsing in a toy shop. While there we saw two brothers playing with a dolls house, then later a brother and sister aged about 11 and 9 respectively. Their dad appeared round the corner and loudly asked, "James are you playing with the DOLLS HOUSE?! CAUGHT YOU!" Having been shamed in front of us the boy mumbled, "No I wasn't," and ran off quickly. The straightjacket of masculine expectation can be very public and very cruel.

8th November 2011

OMFG just seen Littlewoods Xmas advert. Only mothers do Xmas shopping? Not in this house! #pissofflittlewoods

18th November 2011

I notice more and more how, despite my attempts to treat them the same, that I can feel how deeply ingrained my own attitudes are, despite my awareness. I mean in very very subtle ways. If I wasn't so tired I'd try to think of examples.

21st November 2011

Something that is bothering me at the moment is the young age at which children start playing mostly with friends of their own gender. We purposely arrange playdates with our daughter's male peers and they play well, but at nursery I notice the boys names I used to hear have been replaced by girls' names. By age 3 they've been socialised differently to the extent that they are very aware of their differences. I noticed the big difference once she started nursery. Until then, she seemed to mix pretty freely. On first day at nursery a carer said, "Come here and play with the girls" and referred to the car-table as the 'boys corner'.

One of our followers tweeted us about a charity that takes donations for Christmas presents for needy children and has recommendations for giving girls dolls and boys cars. Well it happens that our daughter's granny was doing this at the weekend and got her to help pack one box for a girl and one for a boy. It was a great thrill when she insisted her granny put one of the two cars from the boy's box into the girl's box, saying it wasn't fair. But of course she didn't insist the boy's box should have hairclips in the same way.

23rd November 2011

A voice message from a relative, "Really annoyed, [daughter's] pre-school nativity play and all the girls are angels, boys are shepherds."

3rd December 2011

Justin's House on #Cbeebies. I like the fact the monster is female. Today her cousin, who likes cuddles, visits. He's pink.

9th December 2011

Watching old films with the 3-year-old can be tricky but interesting. *The Rescuers* (1977) sees the lead girl worry she won't be adopted because she thinks she's not pretty enough, as though this is the only reason parents would want a girl. And the mice make a big deal of the fact a female has never been on a mission and it's not really allowed. On the flip side, *Pete's Dragon* (1977) sees the boy sing a song to the dragon called *I Love You Too*. I have my doubts you'd see a song about love sung by a boy in contemporary film. (Examples?)

I tried not to be irritated with a patriarchy-enforcing 3-year-old today. Playing dressing-up at his house he kept insisting that my 3-year-old girl wear a floral orange/pink/purple cloak saying, "It's pink, it's pink, I'm a pirate, you be a princess." I said, "You could wear it?" and he says "I don't like pink." He wanted her to conform to his view of what a girl wears. He kept insisting. Only 3 years old. Gah.

13th December 2011

Listening to Laura Nelson on BBC Radio 5 Live right now, who successfully campaigned for Hamleys to change their in-store signage from 'Girls' and 'Boys'. Her master stroke was calling Hamleys parent company in Iceland where they have stronger views on equality. Thank goodness for Cordelia Fine's amazing book *Delusions of Gender* that can dispel neuro-sexist myths about gender brain differences.

18th December 2011

Prepare to be furious, *Legos For Girls: Lego Friends To Be Released January 2012* (Huffington Post 16th December, 2011). "If it takes color-coding or ponies and hairdressers to get girls playing with Lego, I'll put up with it." >> I won't.

20th December 2011

The gender binary toy divide can be ignored for most of the year in this house, but at Christmas it's right up in your face, grrrrr.

25th December 2011

Things at the @GenderDiary family Christmas have been mercifully free of the need to comment here. A very happy day. Hope yours is peaceful.

3rd January 2012

Bus driver to our 4-year-old: What did you get for Christmas?

She is too shy to say.

Him: Can't remember? I bet you just ripped open your presents and threw them to one side, just like a girl.

Then: I bet you got a doll and a pushchair?

Me: No, Lego and Play-Doh.

Have been told by three different adults over Christmas that you need to get out the house so "the boys" can burn up some energy.

Losing the battle against the blanket use of 'he' for everything (especially animals who are not 'obviously' female). We try to use 'they' 'person' and 'child' etc. The kids' grandmother gave the 4-year-old a toy kangaroo for Christmas which she constantly called 'he', even though it came with a book that called her 'she' and had a baby Joey in her pocket. 4-year-old ended up fluctuating between 'he' and 'she' too. Must say though, the book is a classic example of the kangaroo only being female because she is the mother in the story. All other animals male.

9th January 2012

At the park today, on a roundabout with the kids, a boy stops to look at something. His mother to friend, "He's looking at an ant. He's such a boy."

I need to make a correction. That kangaroo book did have *other* female characters. Phew glad that's sorted, felt we'd been misleading you ;-)

Just found this rather twee, gender-neutral parable (*The Story of X* by Lois Gould). Odd, but thought provoking in parts. Appeared in Ms. Magazine in 1975.

On 10th Jan we've been tweeting for a year. And we're writing a guest piece for The F-word UK.

10th January 2012

Going through a year's worth of tweets shows what great stuff people have brought to our attention. Not getting on very fast, though. I'm just being reminded how the Smurf Movie caused me to froth at the mouth with rage last year. Seriously, one female character in the twenty-first century?

When I tweeted about *The Story of X* by Lois Gould yesterday, calling it twee, I hadn't realised it was a children's story. Someone said they had it in a book as a child and loved it. Makes sense. If you're a non-conforming kid it is a lovely thing to read. The story was in this wonderful looking 1983 book *Stories for Free Children* by Letty Cottin Pogrebin (via @Maureen).

12th January 2012

A text comes in: "Help! [Son]'s school topic is Knights and Princesses! Are there any 'alternative' princess books? Or 'boy' princess ones?" I send links:

My Princess Boy by Cheryl Kilodavis and illustrated by Suzanne DeSimone

Feminism for early starters: Picture books by Treasury Islands 28th February 2011

Six Princess Books for Parents Who Really, Really Hate Princess Books by Tom B on Buildingalibrary.com, 11th January 2012

13th January 2012

Interesting chat with our daughter (when she should've been going to sleep!) on marriage. It suggested we're doing something right. A friend at nursery (girl) has told her a girl can't marry a girl but, she says, "That's not right is it daddy?" I say she's right a girl can marry a girl, boy marry a boy – remind her of married men we know – or, like mummy and daddy, you don't have to get married at all. Says she's going to marry various people at nursery then says, "It depends who falls in love with you. You can fall in love with a girl or a boy and get married. You and mummy fell in love and you're not married and that's OK... I'm going to get married, and have a cake." I say that's fine and I look forward to going to her wedding. NOW GO TO SLEEP. Interesting that she raised it, that she rejected a friend's claim re: same sex marriage. Possibly influence of *The Family Book* Christmas present too?

15th January 2012

RT @mummumbles: @GenderDiary Is there a list of books anywhere for parents of boys who like ballet and dolls and pink?

Presume you've seen My Princess Boy? @mummumbles Will need help from our followers for further ideas…

18th January 2012

Not had any suggestions for books for parents of boys who like ballet and dolls and pink. Anyone?

Yesterday, I set up daughter and friend with a Playmobil castle. I passed him a female figure and said she was important in our game when we play. He said, "Eurghh, I only like knights!" and dropped her. At age 3 he's learnt to dislike any female association in toys. His mother and another were telling me that since being at nursery class at school they've both had invites to play at other children's houses, but both have only had invites from children of the same sex.

22nd January 2012

At a 4-year-old's pirate themed birthday party. Two girls were in shop bought outfits that for some reason crossed princess and pirate costume. Lots of pink. Entertainer led a game of Captain's Coming (port, starboard, etc) including the instruction to go "Ooh la la" when the 'Captain's girlfriend's coming'. Not sure how felt about that. Later our daughter recounted it as saying "Ooh la la" when the Captain's boyfriend is coming. Not sure what that says but probably a good thing.

23rd January 2012

Jeremy Vine (BBC Radio 2) is discussing the gender neutral child story from today's Daily Mail. Buckle up or, better, just avoid. Here's a piece on the child being raised gender-neutral in Cambridgeshire, if you haven't seen it, *Couple raise child as 'gender neutral' to avoid stereotyping* (Daily Telegraph 20th January 2012).

28th January 2012

Hi @alexwinterstv we're very keen on you and Cbeebies, but could you think about not calling all toys 'Mr (animal)'? There are female animals too!

4th February 2012

Freaks me out when we get followed by stuff like @ChoosebabyGender. The fact people want to choose shows the expectations they already have. Finding it hard to fit complicated thoughts about the experiences of our kids into tweets. Got a blog post nearly finished to share soon though.

6th February 2012

I try to keep positive as a parent who wants to see this generation grow-up equal, but things like the #UniLad culture make me want to scream!

7th Febuary 2012

I've had enough of reading the Ladybird book *Stories for 4-year-olds* at bedtime. It has 24 pages, three stories. All three stories are about a male animal. The whole book contains 10 male characters. The only two female characters are 'the vicar's wife' (she can't be a character on her own, she's just an extension of a man) and the other character is the mother of a tortoise, the usual reason a female makes it into a story is because she's the ever present carer. These aren't stories for my 4-year-old girl, Ladybird.

Meanwhile on Facebook a friend has posted a picture of her boy pushing a blue toy pushchair. Comments range from, "It's political correctness gone loop di loop", to someone saying that their son having a pushchair caused "much debate at Christmas... Grandpa's face was a picture." The first comment is a joke. However the fact is that boys with 'girl's' toys are still not an everyday sight.

8th February 2012

We've just popped through the 1,000 followers mark. Thanks to everyone for following. We really like having this space to discuss this stuff.

11th February 2012

Today, like so many times before, in front of the kids, one of these: "That's because he's a boy. Boys are always hungry aren't they." No.

RT @degrassidigest: @GenderDiary Much like girls, they have this persistent need for food

14th February 2012

To a half-term activity afternoon run by the council. Excellent event but… first we made paper flowers. Daughter is asked, "What colour tissue paper do you want?" She says red. Woman says, "Do you want pink?" Then to pottery. Teacher gets us aprons and says to daughter that she has to wear an apron so she doesn't get her beautiful dress mucky. Yes, because girls should be put off fun stuff like pottery for fear of not looking beautiful. No such comments to boys (including me!). Finally, sewing, where you can make a hairband or a bracelet. Opportunity missed to get boys sewing. (I made a bracelet).

17th February 2012

If you missed the BBC Radio 4 *Woman's Hour* piece on the lack of female characters on CBeebies then listen again. We'll tweet a few points. Dr Helen Mott (@BristolFawcett) did a content analysis of a day of CBeebies.[2] In 70% of stories, the action was undertaken by male characters. So of 43 stories that day, only 13 saw the action undertaken by females.

CBeebies' Channel Editor said their research showed slightly more boys than girls watch *Everything's Rosie* and *Fifi and the*

Flower Tots (Channel 5). CBeebies' Editor said the channel is presented with ideas for programmes about male characters more often than female. Dr Mott said, "When children are developing their ideas about gender, CBeebies has a big part to play in reflecting back the reality of the world." Finally, it was interesting to hear the University of Brighton's research on absence of parenting/nurturing fathers in children's picture books.

However I will say the best thing about CBeebies is NO ADVERTS. Adverts perpetuate terrible stereotypes to a much greater extent than most programmes.

So despite being glad CBeebies exists, as there are no adverts, here's some gender gripes. *In the Night Garden* – main characters have a pink/blue binary. Ditto *Waybuloo*. Ditto *Zingzillas*. The time of day we most often watch (7-8am) we see *Postman Pat*, then *Bob the Builder*, then *Timmy Time*. See a pattern? We see three programmes in a row with male leads and that's often all our viewing for a day. Back to back male shouldn't be there.

On the way marketing is training kids to police gender: Earlier the 4-year-old tells me she's colouring with 'girls' colours and seems less than convinced (than when she was younger) when I tell her that "colours are for everyone", as I frequently do. She's mentioned "boys colours" and "girls colours" a few times recently.

Apologies for very UK-centric CBeebies tweeting tonight. We would be pleased to hear about gender representations on channels in other places.

18th February 2012

RT @jakkijax: My 4-year-old nephew won't use pink, red or purple in his pictures and looks at me like I'm mad when I say he can.

That's the state of the nation people. It can't be right.

Took the 4-year-old to the fantastic Hunterian Museum today to look at a brain in a jar (don't ask). The stairs leading to reception were lined with paintings of former Presidents of the Society of Surgeons. Every one a man. This irked me, although I wasn't at all surprised by it. In her play lately she only wants to pretend to be females, sadly. The gender of role models matters.

22nd February 2012

We're both tweeting at the same time from this account. Who knows in what order things will emerge.

In the supermarket our daughter slips on some spaghetti (call the lawyer!). A friendly passer-by says, "Where's your mummy?" and is surprised to see daddy. Because mummies do the shopping or because mummies do the caring for crying children? Or both?

25th February 2012

Sex differences are small compared to the ways we're similar. Obsession with wanting to see us as different makes us so.

Grandparents are staying so sweeping generalisations abound. Yesterday we were told that girls fall out with friends and are meaner to each other.

29th February 2012

Re: the piece we tweeted earlier (*An Interview with Peggy Orenstein on the Gender Trap*, FiveBooks.com, 29th Febraury 2012) it says, "Girls learn the names of Disney princesses before they learn the alphabet". I was amazed last week when our 4-year-old was given a magic flannel (expands in water, so you don't know what will be on it). It was Disney's Cinderella. She knew straight away that it was Cinderella even though it looks different to the original as I remember it. Extra pink bits and larger eyes. Bah!

1st March 2012

The tweet last night about Cinderella and how she looked in the original animation and how she has been updated has set me thinking about the depiction of the shape of women's bodies. The new Cinderella has those very large eyes, like Bratz dolls, and a smaller waist.

5th March 2012

I'm very interested in the way the 4-year-old finds characters in books to choose to 'be'. She'll pick out a person saying, "I'll be that one" and asks me to do the same. She always chooses a figure that looks traditionally female and tries to police the gender of the figure I choose too. I choose figures of the opposite sex to me, or animals, and tell her when you pretend you can be anything you like. She's not convinced. I wonder how far this strong compulsion to only be 'like' the female characters (and therefore what she sees them doing) is influential. Also, if she sees a significantly higher number of male characters, how does this affect the things she thinks about herself?

6th March 2012

RT @catesly: I love how you don't say which of you is tweeting each time too. Adds another dimension re. parents & gender roles

I like that too. It's exactly that kind of anonymity that our kids don't get in the real world, so it's interesting using it here.

My first visit to The Entertainer toy shop today. Oof! I wasn't sure if they were selling toys or sexism. Bricks are for boys so even new 'girls' line of Lego is in the boys section! Pathetic. But given the dearth of toy shops on the high street it'll be unavoidable.

Thanks for the kind words about our The F-word blog. And as we say, it's been wonderful to be able to discuss it with you all here.

(Blog reprinted here)

One Year of the Gender Diary

For a year now we've been tweeting as @GenderDiary about the ways we've seen people treat our 4-year-old girl and our 15-month-old boy differently. We've learnt a lot.

We were inspired to keep the diary by Marianne Grabrucker's book *There's a Good Girl: Gender Stereotyping in the First Three Years – A Diary* (1988). She recorded the experiences in her daughter's life that were shaping her as female. It's a simple but brilliant idea.

When our children were born, people would say, "Oh you'll see, you treat them just the same, but boys and girls act completely differently, it's in the genes." It isn't. And Marianne Grabrucker's book was the thing that showed us how tiny little things in everyday life shape our children's understanding of themselves as being 'boy' or 'girl'.

And it *was* from day one. There was no time for either of our children to show us their 'innate' behaviour because they were already being treated differently. Cards, toys and clothes given to them were different, the language people used about them was different, and there's the fact that we could expect adults to handle our children differently and direct them to different toys depending on their gender, although they are unaware they are doing it.[3]

Other people continually reinforce gender stereotypes that are nothing more than glib generalisations, and within earshot of our children.

A defining moment of the year seems to be to have been the effect being a bridesmaid had on our daughter. We tweeted, "Today we had visitors. Our daughter wanted to wear a bridesmaid's dress she had worn for a friend's wedding. She said she wanted to wear her dress because the visitors "will

78

like me". She was right I suppose. A girl in a frilly dress gets a lot of "don't you look lovely in your pretty dress!" etc. She obviously associates people appreciating her appearance with being liked" (14th January 2011). We don't tweet every time someone comments on our daughter's appearance because we just wouldn't have the time to fit it in.

The fetishisation of all things pink for girls has got to the stage where lazy 'research' and the media tell us that gendered colour preferences have an evolutionary basis, despite them becoming fashionable only 50 years ago.[4]

In contrast we've come to appreciate this year the way boys are quickly socialized into disliking anything that is associated with girls. For example, "Today we saw the second of two different programmes that had a plot on the embarrassment of a male character because he is wearing pink." (26th January 2011)

We've heard many parents bemoan the fact that they've tried not to reinforce gender stereotypes in their kids but still see them develop stereotypical behaviour. They then use this as evidence that gender differences are innate. But gender stereotypes are everywhere and are constantly reinforced. Regardless of our behaviour, our children's experience is made up of so much more than just the words and actions of their parents. They interact with countless adults and children, books, toys, television, images, sights and sounds every day and all these interactions leave their imprint.
The diary has given us a new found awareness that we want to share with other people. You have a document that brings it all together and shows you the weight of it in children's lives. You can then imagine a child's experience as a sort of wall of sound, where dense and complicated layers are built up on a daily basis to make an intricate identity.

It's hard sometimes not to despair and feel the likelihood of change is insurmountable. One of the lovely things about our Twitter account is that our followers share their own experiences, which we retweet, which creates a forum for those equally frustrated by the way children are stereotyped. Like any sort of group, it feels good to know people share your experiences and are struggling against them too.

So let's look to the future and see what we can do. One of the most inspiring things we've seen is by @bluemilk who has run anti-sexism workshops[5] in her child's school. Likewise a teacher who ran gender-awareness sessions[6] with her class while trying to help a pupil come to terms with gender variance is full of good ideas.

And finally, something that F-Word readers are probably already doing. Contradicting people and modelling the alternative. Contradict people when they make glib stereotypical statements, offer them alternative views, tell them your experience is different. Small actions matter.

Diary continued

8th March 2012

If you're a new follower, feel free to tweet your experiences for us to retweet here. It's good to share.

12th March 2012

Was at a kids' interactive exhibition at a gallery on Saturday. They could choose the colour of a slide to put in a projector. A staff member says to a girl, "I bet you'd like to try the pink one wouldn't you?" The girl said yes, like kids do, but didn't sound very convinced. Reinforcement Reinforcement Reinforcement.

Smurf advertising = inwardly seething. Smurfs: Being female is a character trait, and pulling a sexy pose defines this!

The Geena Davis Institute has done some good research on how the media affects girls. Worth following the #girlssavetheworld hashtag tonight.

13th March 2012

Our 2000th tweet shows even we are not immune. In a toy shop I was distraught as son played with dinosaurs, while daughter looked at play high heels, then remembered that before that he was all over the dolls as she looked at a play volcano thing. #swingsandroundabouts

I don't spend all my time in toy shops. But I'm appalled to find Playmobil do those mystery packets in pink for female, blue for male characters.

14th March 2012

BBC Radio 4 Woman's Hour are discussing the power of Twitter to bring feminists together and support each other. That is very much our experience.

Feeling irritated about the lack of female characters in new CBeebies shows considering what the Channel Editor told BBC Woman's Hour recently. Tree Fu Tom is a new favourite with the 4-year-old but I wish the 'gang' wasn't all boys with a token girl.

15th March 2012

Doing this diary has shown me that almost every single thing we do/say/see has an element of gender identity in it.

16th March 2012

I was really surprised to hear this on a nursery rhyme CD earlier: 'Punch and Judy fought for a pie, Punch gave Judy a blow in the eye. Says Punch to Judy, "Will you have more?" Says Judy to Punch, "My eye is too sore."

21st March 2012

Years ago we heard a comedian do a routine about who decides which animals get assigned to boys and which to girls. It's only since becoming parents that it hits home how crazy this 'animal gender policing' is. I've been noticing it particularly on clothes for boys. Animals on boys clothes generally look aggressive and have sharp teeth. Sharks, crocodiles, bears, monsters. So you don't see butterflies, cats, ponies, rabbits. They just don't have sharp enough teeth and they're just not AGRESSIVE enough. It's tedious.

On a related note, the 1-year-old was given pyjamas with football playing monkeys on them before he could walk. Clothes frequently play out assumptions about gender roles.

Toys are the same. So fascinating how it's not the toy but the signifiers on the toy like colour, pattern, texture and teeth (!) that tells the child whether the toy is appropriate for them or not. Free choice? Pah!

29th March 2012

I'm in the middle of making a list of 'feminist' children's books which we'll post here, which may be good for future gifts.

2nd April 2012

Spent an unpleasant few minutes on Clarks Shoes website. It's so heavily divided by gender that you can't search outside boy/girl categories.

.@clarksshoes It's a shame that searching for kids' shoes on your website can only be done by gender. Would you consider reviewing this?

3rd April 2012

This great piece on how men and women authors are treated differently, *On the Rules of Literary Fiction for Men and Women* (The New York Times, 30th March 2012) just reinforces our experience of how boys are socialised from day one to believe the 'female sphere' is not for them i.e 'girls' books/toys are 'other' and shameful to read/play with. But as Meg Wolitzer says in the NY Times piece. It's the publishers/booksellers who enforce the segregation.

6th April 2012

Discovery of unedited German fairy tales where the brave and clever children are as likely to be girls as boys *(The Anti-Grimm*, The Economist, 4th April 2012). Ace. Never been a traditional fairy tale fan but looking forward to this: "The princess slashes her way out of the witches belly and claims her prince."

9th April 2012

Freakish coincidence occurred today when @GenderDiary and @Keris happened to be in the same castle. Real world/Twitterverse collision.

In that castle, a man at the door told our 4-year-old "You can dress-up as a princess". I presume he was telling boys they could be knights. Activities for princesses and knights included making a clay tile, and they could choose a cutter for the shape, she was offered a butterfly, heart or star. Lots of others to choose from but those were princess shapes I presume. Next, making a wand and when choosing colours a dad pipes up that he knows his girl will choose pink. Ours heard that and chose something pinkish. All just general reinforcement of roles but today brought home why history is so difficult as a feminist because most images and narratives we've seen/heard today were about men. To be fair to the castle we visited, they had great activities and they weren't divided for boys and girls in any way other than by costume. It was only individual people who chose to direct the children in certain ways. History itself is something they can't change of course, but it would be so nice to see some imagination in the teaching of history in terms of women.

13th April 2012

Have been in a wifi/mobile-coverage black hole for nearly a week. Nice to be back in an un-tweet-restricted place. What have we missed?

17th April 2012

Going to get this feminist reading list for kids finished this week. All recommendations welcome. Will aim to update it regularly too. And just to say, the list is from pre-school through to teenage, so all suggestions welcome. Older kids especially as that's a bit thin at the moment. We'd be interested to hear whether you edit books while you're reading aloud. I know I do.

An interesting test on school gender policing: A nephew has a school project for which he must dress as an elf or fairy. He has a fairy costume he loves and went in that. This morning his parents reported the teacher said two other boys would be in fairy costumes as well. This evening he says there were no other boys dressed like him and children laughed at him. However they have to wear it again tomorrow and he seems more than happy to do that. I wonder what happened to the expected other two boys. Will request the teacher is asked.

Ah sorry if I gave the impression I'm critical of the school/teacher, no if anything I'd expect it was the two boys or their parents who changed their minds. But I'm going to get my nephew's parents to ask the teacher if they know why they didn't come as fairies. But I understand the dilemma. Parents want to protect their children from being teased for being different, so encourage conformity. Very interesting though, to imagine the number of boys/girls/parents who are modifying their appearance.

Inside Health on BBC Radio 4 now are going to discuss naming genitals. Will listen with interest. Fandango has fallen out of favour here.

19th April 2012

To the body confidence awards at parliament. I'm the only one with a beard in the room I think. Make yourself known! No surprise Caitlin Moran is the first winner. Next Award: I'm uneasy about a MAN saying how he hands down confidence to women through his beauty products. Corporate awards are picked up by men. Awkward. Body confidence is important. So is having senior women in business. Gender Diary favourites (and new friends) Pink Stinks win. Dove win the Body Confidence Award for advertising. What do we think of that?

Great to meet Cerrie Burnell of UK Feminista at Body Confidence Awards tonight hosted by ace as always Jo Swinson. Particularly inspired by what Pink Stinks UK have achieved and looking forward to possible collaboration. Or at least wine in south east London. Forgot to mention Brushed Off. They're very slick and look forward to writing for them.

21st April 2012

This is how it's accepted *and* normal in our culture that boys must be ashamed of owning an object 'meant' for girls, *London 2012: Cyclist Sir Chris Hoy's first bicycle was a girl's bike* (BBC News Online, 17th April 2012). Socialisation of boys to be ashamed of being connected to anything conventionally assigned to girls can only lead to bad things right? For everyone. Surely it leads to boys seeing the 'female' domain as inferior and associated with shame. And females to inferior status. I know I'm stating the bleedin' obvious but small things rankle the biggest sometimes.

22nd April 2012

One of my problems with make-up at age two is that it's a method of getting consumers primed to buy unnecessary shit for life, super young.

26th April 2012

In a blog on how the world denies our daughters @lulasticblog asks whether to "reject all pink, princesses and beauty?" What do you think? It's a good question because we're keen not to encourage the socialisation of kids to see 'female' things as inferior, so it's a fine line between keeping pink toys that reinforce gender stereotypes away from your girls and reinforcing the idea that things 'for girls' are lesser.

29th April 2012

Got a list of diary things we need to tweet but am too knackered. Will see if the other half of the diary will oblige.

30th April 2012

So just a quick tweet about films. Broke the rule about having to see a kids' film with a female lead every other time, but jeez the rain. *Happy Feet Two*, what a mess. From the Gender Diary perspective, almost no female characters other than Gloria who gets stuck in a hole so can't participate in any of the action. There is one baby girl penguin who goes to bring help from another colony, but the action doesn't follow her while she does it, so it's just a footnote in the film. I counted 10 main male characters and two female. Adult female penguins only featured as love interests (to be sleazed over) or mothers and took no part in the action whatsoever. Hated it. Only upside to *Happy Feet Two* was the fact that it depicts fathers looking after their children. But frankly I'm being kind here. Baby girl penguins gyrating was one of the big low points in a very low-pointy film.

1st May 2012

Here's that reading list for kids we've been promising. Lots of alternative princess books for those who need help in that area.

(List reprinted here)

Reading list for kids age 0-14

This is a crowd-sourced list of books, so we haven't read them all, but they've been recommended as suitable to show kids there is more than one way to live life. It's a loosely feminist list with a bit of other gender related reading thrown in. There are plenty of stories for those who prefer a princess who fights the dragon herself. We hope it's helpful. If you'd like to suggest books to add to the list then tweet us @GenderDiary. We've been given permission to include other small lists compiled by @armyofdave and @treasuryislands so thanks very much to them.

Pre-school age

Fix It! illustrated by Georgie Birkett

A chatty, interactive text and merry illustrations encourage both girls and boys to engage in their first 'real' tasks.

The Shy Creatures by David Mack

What does a shy girl want to be when she grows up? A doctor, but not just any doctor — this little girl wants to care for creatures who may seem intimidating, but are really very shy, just like she is.

The Paper Bag Princess by Robert Munsch, illustrated by Michael Martchenko

A princess uses her wit to outsmart a dragon in order to rescue the prince. The prince, seeing that the princess only has a paper bag for clothes, refuses to leave with her. The princess then tells the prince he "looks like a real bum" and they do not get married. The classic anti-princess book.

My Princess Boy by Cheryl Kilodavis

Dyson loves the colour pink and sparkly things. Sometimes he wears dresses and sometimes he wears jeans. He likes to wear his princess tiara, even when climbing trees. He's a Princess Boy.

The Knitting Gorilla by Giles Andreae

After six daughters, the Big Gorilla had a son. "You will grow up to be BIG and FIERCE, just like your daddy!" he said proudly. But the Little Gorilla grew up to be...small...and gentle...and not like his daddy at all. And what he liked doing most...was knitting.

Free to be...You and Me by Marlo Thomas

The original, innovative book that celebrates diversity, challenges stereotypes and encourages kids to be themselves in a joyful, positive manner, through a collection of songs, poems and stories to be read aloud.

My Name Is Not Isabella by Mike Litwin and Jennifer Fosberry

My name is not Isabella explores some of the amazing women who changed history including Rosa Parks (It's from the US) and the reader's mum!

The Little Book of Farmyard Tales by Heather Amery

Mrs Boot is a farmer. She lives on her farm with her two children, Poppy and Sam, and a dog called Rusty. A welcome alternative to the 'farmer's wife' trope. Features a little yellow duck to find on every page.

Where's The Bus? by Eileen Browne

I'm told this is the first ever animal picture book with all female characters. Can it be true? We're very happy for you to tell us otherwise because we'll add the examples to the list. Young children will love to spot all the buses in the illustrations – which the animals miss because they are too busy doing something else.

Don't You Dare, Dragon! by Annie Kubler

All Dragon wants to do is cool down and have a little fun, but every time she tries, she ruins it for everyone else! Thankfully, she finds some friends who need exactly what Dragon does best. A book about a female dragon with an integral finger puppet for added fun.

I'm Not Scared! by Jonathan Allen

Baby Owl is out for a moonlight stroll through the woods but each animal he bumps into tells him not to be scared. Some of those animals are female, which is unusual, and baby owl's carer is his dad, who puts him to bed. You don't often see fathers in picture books.

Big Noisy Machines – Digger by Sue Hendra

Children will love imagining they are driving a big noisy digger with this fun interactive book. The bright, bold illustrations and simple text are accompanied with a noisy sound chip that allows readers to get involved with all the work on the busy building site. Women and men operate the machinery.

Age 4-8 (Can be read to younger children)

Handy Girls Can Fix it by Peggy Kahn (Reading Age: 4+)

A group of girls form a club to fix things. Some paint, some build doghouses, and they get satisfaction helping people by working with their hands.

Amazing Grace by Mary Hoffman (Reading Age: 4+)

When her school decides to perform Peter Pan, Grace is longing to play Peter, but her classmates say that Peter was a boy, and besides, he wasn't black...But Grace's Ma and Nana tell her she can be anything she wants if she puts her mind to it.

Princess Grace by Mary Hoffman (Reading Age: 4+)

Grace has the chance to be a princess in a school parade but what does a princess do, apart from wearing beautiful clothes and looking pretty? With the help of her teacher she learns about warrior princesses such as Pin-Yang of China who started a woman's army, and Amina of Nigeria who led warriors into battle. Eventually Grace decides that she wants to dress in West African Kente robes and says: "I feel like a proper princess – ready for an adventure".

Mirette on the High Wire by Emily Arnold McCully (Reading Age: 4+)

Best summed up by the first reviewer on Amazon: "How many children's books do you know where the girl (rather than a boy or an animal) saves the day by doing something heroic? Relatively few come to my mind. I was delighted to find this wonderful tale of 19th century entertainment fits that bill. Ms. McCully had originally set out to write a biography of the famous tightrope walker Blondin, when she decided to write this book instead. The Mirette character is based on her own recollections of being a brave girl."

Zog by Julia Donaldson (Reading Age: 4+)

At Dragon School, Zog tries his best with all of his lessons, but he keeps having accidents. Luckily, every time he gets into a scrape a mysterious girl comes along and fixes him up. Finally, Zog has to attempt the hardest task of all – capturing a princess – and finds that he's not very good at it. He's feeling very sorry for himself when along comes the girl again – can she save the day this time?

Kate and the Beanstalk by Mary Pope Osborne (Reading Age: 4+)

A clever twist on a classic fairy tale. A clever young girl climbs the beanstalk, outwits the giant and brings home riches to her mother.

Horace And Morris But Mostly Dolores by James Howe (Reading Age: 4+)

Horace, Morris, and Dolores do everything together and know that they will be Friends Forever, until one day, when Horace and Morris become part of an exclusive boys' club and Dolores finds herself left out. Soon she too finds her own club, where no boys are allowed and girls are supposed to have fun doing girl stuff. But after a while, Horace and Morris and Dolores realise they aren't happy at all doing what everyone in their clubs seems to enjoy. They miss each other. Is it too late to be friends again?

Girls Are Not Chicks Coloring Book by Julie Novak and Jacinta Bunnell (Reading Age: 4+)

This book helps to "deconstruct the homogeneity of gender expression in children's media by showing diverse pictures that reinforce positive gender roles for girls". Girls are not chicks. Girls are thinkers, creators, fighters, healers and superheroes.

Cinder Edna by Ellen Jackson (Reading Age: 4+)

Cinder Edna was forced to work for her wicked stepmother and stepsisters, just like her neighbour, Cinderella. But while Cinderella had the good fortune to be rescued by her fairy godmother, Edna was strong, self-reliant, spunky – and she lived happier ever after.

Piggybook By Anthony Browne (Reading Age: 4+)

Mr Piggott and his two sons behave like pigs to Mrs Piggott until she walks out. Left to fend for themselves, the male Piggotts undergo some curious changes.

Girls Will Be Boys Will Be Girls Will Be... By Jacinta Bunnell, Irit Reinheimer (Reading Age: 4+)

Girls Will be Boys Will be Girls pokes fun at the tired constraints of gender normativity and makes it okay to step outside the lines.

Princess Smartypants by Babette Cole (Reading Age: 4+)

Princess Smartypants does NOT want to get MARRIED. She enjoys being a Ms but being a rich and pretty princess means that all the princes want her to be their Mrs. Find out how Princess Smartypants fights to preserve her independence in this fairlytale with a difference...

Prince Cinders by Babette Cole (Reading Age: 4+)

Prince Cinders leads a very hard life. Bullied by his three hairy brothers about his less than perfect looks, he spends all his time cleaning and tidying up after them. One Saturday night Prince Cinders' luck changes as a small, dirty fairy falls down the chimney and promises that his wishes shall come true. Not all the fairy's spells turn out as planned.

The Tough Princess by Martin Waddell and Patrick Benson
(Reading Age: 4+)

This book turns the traditional fairy tale rules on their heads
and recreates the genre in a clear and clever way without
confusing the young.

Jane and the Dragon by Martin Baynton (Reading Age: 4+)

Jane longs to be a knight, but everyone laughs at her.
Everyone, that is, except the court jester, who lends her a
small suit of armour to help make her dream come true. And
when an enormous dragon swoops in and steals the prince,
Jane quickly gets the chance to prove herself!

Daddy's Roommate by Michael Willhoite (Reading Age: 4+)

This story's narrator begins with his parent's divorce and
continues with the arrival of "someone new at Daddy's
house." The new arrival is male. This new concept is
explained to the child as "just one more kind of love."

Heather Has Two Mommies by Leslea Newman (Reading Age:
4+)

Heather's favourite number is two. She has two arms, two
legs, two eyes, two ears, two hands, and two feet. Heather
also has two mommies, Mama Jane and Mama Kate.

Clever Polly And The Stupid Wolf by Catherine Storr (Reading
Age: 5+)

A very popular classic. Polly continually outsmarts the wolf
in his elaborate schemes. Polly has a plan that's bound to foil
the stupid wolf.

The Great Big Book of Families by Mary Hoffman (Reading Age: 5+)

What is a family? Once, it was said to be a father, mother, boy, girl, cat and dog living in a house with a garden. As times have changed, families have changed too. An optimistic look at families of today.

10,000 Dresses by Marcus Ewert (Reading Age: 5+)

Bailey dreams about beautiful dresses and longs to make them and wear them. "You're a BOY!" Mother and Father tell Bailey. "You shouldn't be thinking about dresses at all." Bailey meets Laurel, an older girl who is touched and inspired by Bailey's imagination and courage. In friendship, the two of them begin making dresses together.

The Princess and the Dragon by Audrey Wood (Reading Age: 5+)

When a princess who behaves like a dragon meets a dragon who behaves like a princess, they realise the best thing to do is change roles. The Princess enjoys her life playing devilish tricks upon unsuspecting old knights and the dragon enjoys ballet and playing the piano.

The Big Brother by Stephanie Dagg (Reading Age: 5+)

Will Dara know what to do when the new baby comes? If only he could have a doll to practise. A challenge to gendered ideas about children's toys. Funny and heart-warming.

Captain Abdul's Pirate School By Colin McNaughton (Reading Age: 5+)

This is the story (in diary form) of reluctant pirate pupil, Pickles. At Captain Abdul's awful academy Pickles is taught essential pirate topics such as how to make cannon balls and the correct way to say, "Ooh arrgh!" Discovering a plot to kidnap the pupils and hold them to ransom, Pickles leads a daring mutiny. Pickles is revealed on the last page to be a girl called Maisy.

The Princesses Have a Ball by Teresa Bateman (Reading Age: 6+)

The king is puzzled. Why aren't his 12 daughters dreaming of princes? Subversive (and rhyming) high jinks by sporty princesses with attitude. The ball they have is a baseball.

Rickshaw Girl by Mitali Perkins (Reading Age: 7+)

Saleem can drive a rickshaw and help earn money for his family. Naima longs to help but is forbidden as a girl. A wonderfully unique story set in rural Bangladesh exploring the challenges change brings.

Matilda by Roald Dahl (Reading Age: 7+)

At age five Matilda can do double-digit multiplication problems and blitz-read Dickens but what she would really like is parents who are loving and understanding, but hers are not. Matilda invents a game of punishing her parents when they treat her badly and she discovers that she has supernatural powers.

Bill's New Frock by Anne Fine (Reading Age: 7+)

Bill's New Frock offers young male readers insight into how people treat you differently when you're female. Bill Simpson wakes up to find he's a girl, and his mother makes him wear a pink dress to school. How on earth is he going to survive a whole day like this? Everything just seems to be different for girls.

Petronella by Jay Williams (Reading Age: 8+)

Princess Petronella challenges the mysterious enchanter Albion for a prince's freedom. She attempts a daring escape – but is she rescuing the right man? A modern fantasy classic, full of wit and surprise, with an admirable heroine.

Girls Think of Everything: Stories of Ingenious Inventions by Women by Catherine Thimmesh (Reading Age: 8+)

In kitchens and living rooms, in garages and labs and basements, even in converted chicken coops, women and girls have come up with ingenious innovations that have made our lives simpler and better. What inspired these women and just how did they turn their ideas into realities?

The Wrestling Princess and Other Stories by Judy Corbalis and Helen Craig (Reading Age: 8+)

Six stories, each about a girl who pursues interests such as driving a forklift truck, fighting dragons or piloting a helicopter, as well as a hungry monster, a pink elephant and a magic parrot.

My Naughty Little Sister by Dorothy Edwards (Reading Age: 8+)

My naughty little sister is full of mischief. She tries to cut off the cat's tail, she bites Father Christmas's hand, and eats all of the trifle with Bad Harry at his party.

Ramona the Pest by Beverly Cleary, illustrated by Tracy Dockray (Reading Age: 8+)

Ramona the Pest shows us a mischievous girl's perspective on the trials and delights of beginning school. In this book Ramona is age 5, follow the series right through until the final book, Ramona's World, when she turns 10.

The Ordinary Princess by M M Kaye (Reading Age: 8+)

The youngest of seven princesses is given the gift of being ordinary. When her parents start turning to desperate measures to get her married, Amy runs away to live in the forest with her companions, a squirrel and a crow. This happy existence is interrupted by the deterioration of Amy's clothes. In order to purchase new ones, Amy gets a job as a kitchen maid at the castle in a neighbouring kingdom and makes an unexpected friend.

Pippi Longstocking by Astrid Lindgren (Reading Age: 8+)

Children's classic. Pippi lives without grown-ups in Villa Villekulla with a horse, a monkey and a big suitcase full of gold coins. The grown-ups in her village try to make Pippi behave in ways that they think a little girl should but Pippi has other ideas. She would much rather spend her days arranging wild, exciting adventures to enjoy with her neighbours, Tommy and Annika, or entertaining everyone she meets with her outrageous stories.

Age 9-12

Seesaw Girl by Linda Sue Park (Reading Age: 9+)

In 17th century Korea, girls from "good" families stay within the Inner Court until they are married but Jade yearns to glimpse the world outside these walls. Will she realise her dream?

Girls are Best by Sandi Toksvig (Reading Age: 9+)

Women gladiators, women in the Bayeaux Tapestry, women inventors – Sandi Toksvig uncovers them all in her light-hearted approach to the serious message of this book:

women have always done amazing things but have mostly been overlooked by history.

His Dark Materials Trilogy: Northern Lights, Subtle Knife, Amber Spyglass by Philip Pullman (Reading Age: 9+)

Beginning in Oxford, this story takes Lyra and her animal-daemon Pantalaimon on a dangerous rescue mission to the ice kingdoms of the far north, where she begins to learn about the mysterious particles they call Dust, a substance for which a terrible war between different worlds will be fought. Has won the UK's top awards for children's literature.

The Turbulent Term of Tyke Tiler by Gene Kemp (Reading Age: 9+)

The book tells the story of its main characters' final term at Cricklepit Combined School. It is principally narrated by 'Tyke' Tiler, a bold and athletic 12-year-old with the reputation of being a troublemaker. Up to the end of the penultimate chapter the narrative is written without revealing the protagonist's gender, and the daring nature of Tyke's exploits often leads readers to assume Tyke is a boy. The story ends with the revelation that Tyke is female and her full name Theodora.

Bridge To Terabithia by Katherine Paterson (Reading Age: 9+)

Jess pushes himself to win the year's first school-yard race but his victory is stolen by newcomer Leslie, a girl, who didn't even know enough to stay on the girls' side of the playground. Leslie completely changes his worldview about what girls can and can't do and how they're "supposed" to be. It is Leslie who invents Terabithia, the secret country on an island across the creek.

The Tales of Beedle the Bard by JK Rowling (Reading Age: 9+)

This is here as part of the alternative-princess meme. The Tales of Beedle the Bard are the fairy tales that witches and wizards read to their kids and which have a role in assisting Harry Potter in his quests against Voldemort. "You won't find any princesses sitting around waiting to be rescued in there."

Dealing with Dragons by Patricia C. Wrede (Reading Age: 10+)

Princess Cimerone and the dragon Kazul share a spirited adventure with an extraordinary cast of characters in this first book in the *Enchanted Forest Chronicles* series.

The Hero and the Crown by Robin McKinley (Reading Age: 10+)

There is no place in the country of Damar for Aerin, daughter of a witch-woman, who is also the king's daughter; and so she befriends her father's crippled war-horse, Talat, and teases her cousin Tor into teaching her to handle a sword. Aerin rediscovers the old recipe for dragonfire-proof kenet, and when the army is called away to the other side of the country, it is she who, alone but for Talat, rides out to confront Maur, the Black Dragon, the last of the Great Dragons, for centuries thought dead.

A Hat Full Of Sky by Terry Pratchett (Reading Age: 12+)

Terry Pratchett's second Tiffany Aching novel. She previously saved the world from the Queen of the Elves and is about to discover that battling evil monarchs is child's play compared to mortal combat with a Hiver. At 11-years-old, she is the boldest heroine ever to have confronted the Forces of Darkness while armed with a frying pan.

Parrotfish by Ellen Wittlinger (Reading Age: 12+)

Parrotfish can serve as an introduction to transgender issues for curious readers. Angela changes her name to Grady, and begins to live as a boy, and though his family and friends initially have trouble accepting the change, he does find support from them and one particular teacher.

Dolltopia by Abby Denson (Reading Age: 12+)

A Barbie-like doll suffers a crisis once she realizes her fate is to live in a dream house and marry a boring, Ken-like doll. So what does she do? She breaks free, gets a punk haircut and makes her way to Dolltopia, a land full of rebel dolls who refuse to live lives that were planned out for them.

Spindle's End by Robin McKinley (Reading Age: 14+)

An inventive retelling of Sleeping Beauty but featuring a heroine who is anything but passive – she prefers leather breaches to ball gowns, can communicate with animals and saves herself and her village from the sleeping enchantment.

Shadows on the Moon by Zoe Marriott (Reading Age: 14+)

16-year-old Suzume is able to recreate herself in any form. But who is she really? A powerful tale of magic, love and revenge with a strong female lead, set in fairy-tale Japan.

Zoe Marriot is a follower of @GenderDiary and picked out this one in particular for this list, but take a look at all her books.

Adults Reading

There's a Good Girl: Gender Stereotyping in the First Three Years – A Diary by Marianne Grabrucker

The Book that inspired @GenderDiary.

Further Resources

A Mighty Girl is the world's largest collection of books and movies for parents, teachers, and others dedicated to raising smart, confident, and courageous girls.

Letterbox Library is a children's booksellers celebrating equality and diversity.

Diary continued

2nd May 2012

Happy to hear any feedback about the list and any further suggestions.

RT @EssexMums: Gender-reveal cakes? What do you think? ("*celebrations at which friends and family gather around an expectant mother to find out the sex of her child, through the cutting of a cake that contains pink sponge for a girl, and blue for a boy.*")

Well the upsetting fact about gender reveal cakes is that parents who consider the sex of their child to be very important will also have preconceived ideas about what a girl or boy should be, which will limit those children.

Would be interested to hear what you think of Sweden's gender-neutral pronoun 'hen' (*Will Sweden abolish the concept of gender?* iO9.com, 5th January 2012). I think it's a great idea and so was asking to see what opposition people might have to it. At home we talk about people, person, they, and children where possible.

3rd May 2012

Yesterday, 18-month-old's childminder: "He really loves to dance, I've never known a child who likes to dance so much... for a boy."

9th May 2012

Queen's speech in UK today. The Government announcing plans for shared parental leave. See Rebecca Asher's book *Shattered: Modern Motherhood and the Illusion of Equality* for why this is so important! What the Government's plans are and whether they'll be any good remains to be seen. But any move towards more equal sharing of childcare is a good step.

Happy to have just used our book list to choose a birthday present for 9-year-old nephew!

12th May 2012

Good idea: "Girlguiding UK say they are… to create a series of "day in the life" videos, featuring successful women in a range of careers."

15th May 2012

Another distracting headline for a piece that has some useful stats, *Are Dads the New Moms?* (The Wall Street Journal, 11th May 2012). "Phasing out… gendered roles of "husband and wife" and "father and mother" and replacing them with the… roles of "spouse and parent."

Something we've obviously mentioned before is the constant naming of animals as 'he' in kids' books. Am now equally irritated by noticing animals are only female when there are baby animals around. There are not many examples to the contrary. The reinforcement of females only as carers of children and then males being absent is standard. As much as I love Bookstart, our kid was given *No! Says Olly Bear*. It's awful. A father bear is present but the book screams: LOOKING AFTER CHILDREN IS A WOMAN'S JOB! It opens with mum giving kids breakfast and encouraging them to play nicely. On page 5 Dad appears to ask who's coming to the shops. Olly is. "I'll come too, with the baby" says mum. She's always seen pushing a buggy, providing food, caring. When they get home Olly "wouldn't help Mum unpack the shopping." Her job obviously. She appears on 11 pages of the book, the Dad on 6. It's Copyright 2003 FFS.

19th May 2012

RT @Keris: @GenderDiary Sorry it's so dark, but...

[Keris tweets a photo of *The Usborne Cookbook for Boys* which has meat on the cover and *The Usborne Cookbook for Girls* which has cakes and biscuits on the cover]

Gonna say something profound here. See that cooking books for boys/girls photo, I just want a world that has "stuff for people". Am I wrong? I just want my kids to be able to *choose* if that f'ing cooking book with cupcakes is the one they want, not be told their sex means it *is*. It's silly to be raging here about f'ing cupcakes when some live with gendercide, but the tiniest things are the building bricks of misogyny. It just means you have to (if you have children of different sexes) buy two. That's all it's about. Making more money. Milking our kids.

20th May 2012

Our 4-year-old just watched *Barney's Barrier Reef* on BBC2. Every single one of about 15 animals was referred to as 'he'. It's also presented by a man and a woman, but only he gets his name in the title. I say to the 4-year-old, "I can't believe this programme. Not all animals are he". She says there is one kind of animal that is always a he, "Dinosaurs".

26th May 2012

Just looking at activities to book for our upcoming week at Center Parcs. Fairy and Wizard Academy. Not separate sessions, kids must be either/or. Could be some furious tweeting next week.

A book read to our 18-month-old at bedtime is all about animals (*Say Goodnight to the Sleepy Animals*, by Ian Whybrow). There is only one female – a cat with kittens! Of course the animals weren't male when *I* read it. When the 4-year-old can read it'll be hard!

Kids' books and gender representation is something we come back to frequently here. Being aware is half the battle. I often look at books and can see it's not something that has crossed the author or publisher's mind. Children are learning through books/TV/films where females are never seen at the 50% they represent. It sends them a message.

On another note, there's a very interesting study by (I think) University of Brighton on fathers being absent from picture books. [7]

31st May 2012

Good report on *Channel 4 News* on how Jessica Ennis (Olympic Heptathlon Champion) being called fat is part of girls' reluctance to play sport.

2nd June 2012

What do you think of this toy, Roominate, aimed at girls? Design and build a toy house complete with circuit for electrics. In an ideal world we'd prefer non-gendered marketing, but in the face of the tidal wave of socialisation into gendered-play, is this needed? The question I've been asking myself today is whether you have to work with the situation we've got? Very unsure. As @MituK said "it only reinforces gender-segregated toys, but then again, it is a pragmatic solution". Thoughts?

3rd June 2012

The release of Disney's *Brave* will make sticking to our rule (that every other film we take our 4-year-old to see must have a female lead) easier. Yay. Hoping *Brave* will live up to expectations. The lead looks kickass. And the 4-year-old will love the bow and arrowing (as she calls it).

9th June 2012

Hello to new followers. Thanks for following and please do get involved in the conversation, and tweet us your experiences. In other news… Apologies the actual diary side of this has been a bit absent. Will tweet it all soon. Also writing a monthly blog for @bea_magazine soon.

10th June 2012

Some actual diary incoming.

The 18-month-old has started to say 'man'. It's no surprise the word comes before 'woman', which is harder to say, and much less used. But he's surrounded by the word man in so many ways. The green man at the traffic lights, so many songs – This Old Man, The Muffin Man, Five Little Men in a Flying Saucer, I am the Music Man. All these are sung every week at playgroups and on our CDs. Everything is a man. Meanwhile, I noticed earlier all our (small) Lego figures are male apart from the single one our 4-year-old made up herself in a Lego store. So we have a ratio of eight male to one female. The Duplo we have is much better and came with women in the packs. Lego for older kids goes off course. And on the Lego, annoying that the single female figure was bought at our child's instigation and can only be done in the Lego shop itself.

The kids' grandmother was telling me why it's easier to put our 4-year-old in a dress (while she's sitting there), she says, "Then they're less inclined to play at getting muddy knees". When I protest that this stops them playing freely, she accepts this is a bit of a shame. But says girls don't keep playing in that mucky way that boys do, as they get older.

D'ya think the first thing you said might be part of the reason?! To be clear, I'm not blaming dresses for the fact girls can be less active. It's just one of the factors in how they are treated differently. Adult attitudes to clothes, from keeping clean, to enforcing modesty (if pants visible), to more interest in appearance, could affect play.

16th June 2012

Language. Earlier at the kids' sports group someone asks me how old the 19-month-old is and said he was "boisterous". I replied that he was big for his age. The comment was meant very kindly as she was laughing and pointing out how happy he was but for me that word wasn't right. He's confident, especially when he's with his sibling but they're very gentle kids. I put the word down to shorthand for 'a boy having fun'. The language people use about each of them can be very different.

Every time that reading list gets favourited or retweeted I'm amused about all those unseen children reading. We'll be updating our list soon as well (which you can always find via the link on our twitter profile) and writing a blog post about books.

18th June 2012

Earlier a dress for a wedding we're going to arrived in the post. Our 4-year-old got very excited when I tried it on and wanted to join in by trying on a dress and shoes. She stood in front of the mirror, and repeated something she's said before, "People will like me, like this". I ask her first if she likes it. I say that what she thinks is more important than what other people think. Then I tell her whatever she's wearing she's wonderful. She agrees that I love her whatever. Then says, "But some *other* people will like me and think I'm pretty like this too". I understand it feels good when people compliment her on her appearance but it's so often the first thing they say, so as Lisa Bloom says, "I always bite my tongue when I meet little girls, restraining myself from my first impulse, which is to tell them how darn cute/pretty/beautiful/well-dressed/well-manicured well-coiffed they are." (*How to talk to little girls*, Huffington Post, 22nd June, 2012) I find it difficult that girls are more aware of it than boys because people give them more praise for their appearance. I can't remember who (but someone on Twitter) said every day they intentionally compliment a woman on something other than her appearance. The intention was to make women feel good about themselves for their achievements/intelligence rather than their appearance.

Interesting or just a thing? So our daughter doesn't have an imaginary friend, she has two imaginary dogs: Snuffle and Sniff. Today I learned that Snuffle is male, Sniff female. The story went that Snuffle was lost, had gone back to previous owner, was a naughty dog. Sniff on the other hand has a pretty bow and a necklace. Sadly I think this is reflective of stories she hears – males are active, females are pretty.

19th June 2012

An Ofsted report finds pupils are encouraged to express themselves and to dress as opposite sex without judgement. The shame about that very positive Ofsted report is the way it is being reported. I daren't look at the Daily Mail for obvious reasons.

Some thoughts on our own unintentional prejudices. This morning our 19-month-old wanted to put hairclips in his hair. He was wearing them when our 4-year-old came in and said, "Those aren't for him!" I immediately assumed she meant the hairclips, but only asked, "What?" She had been referring to something he was holding and she never mentioned the clips at all. Clearly they had been prominent in my mind when I looked at him. But they were unremarkable to her. Good. But not so good on my part. One clip fell out at breakfast and I took the other one out without thinking about it before he went to his childminder. A lot of this stuff is wedged in tight to the recesses of the mind.

One of Gender Diary met the ace Dr Laura Nelson (@DrLauraNelson) earlier, who is running the Breakthrough Stereotypes project. Hoping there are ways that us and you can help get the project into other schools. If there is, we will let you know.

20th June 2012

Remembered something I forgot to tweet about the meeting in parliament last night. It was on equality in science and engineering. There was a group of school girls, one of whom said she had told her careers adviser she wanted to be an astronaut, but she understood it wasn't very practical. All the fab women in the room told her she absolutely could do it and gave her tips on approaching NASA. Ace stuff.

21st June 2012

Have you seen this Atlantic article on work/life balance, *Why Women Still Can't Have It All* by Anne-Marie Slaughter (13th June 2012). You read my mind. Men's role is totally what's missing. She fails to consider what legislation could make it possible either. But I think that's a very US way of examining the issue (to look to business to change), whereas my mind goes straight to policy. I think it's helpful though. Much more nuanced than most pieces on the subject. It's a shame how she asks if men are going to be prepared to take the same pauses in their careers. She should be telling them!

23rd June 2012

Interesting that the 19-month-old already sees the difference between the children labelled in a book as 'boy' (short hair, wearing shorts and t-shirt) and 'girl' (long hair, wearing a dress). He says "man" and "sister".

27th June 2012

Dear publishing industry, What's the secret formula for deciding which pieces of classic literature aren't for girls? [Tweeted with a photo of the Waverley Books *Classic Story Collection for Boys*, which includes *Around the World in 80 Days* and *Gulliver's Travels*].

Some news from the kids' aunt about their 5-year-old cousin. He wants to get pink Crocs (shoes) for summer but said, "I know I'd never be able to wear them to school because everyone would laugh at me." He says he knows he's not meant to like pink but he doesn't care that it's a girl's colour. Ack, where to start unpicking those sad statements? To sum up: one colour represents all girls, and girls are shameful for boys to be similar to. Our culture socialises boys to reject anything associated with girls, yet people wonder why boys won't read books/watch TV and films with a female lead. Ffs. It must be so confusing.

It's just so frustrating that kids are constantly having their choices prescribed for them by gender. We found having kids was a real eye opener. If you're finding the same, then we hope you'll get involved in the conversation.

2nd July 2012

Gender reading gap 'not biological' – girls get more books (*Gender reading gap 'not biological'*, London Evening Standard, 2nd July 2012) I'd expect the result that girls are given more books and encouraged more. Adults lack awareness that they treat girls and boys differently.

"Teachers who pick texts that appeal to girls, a lack of books in the home and an expectation that they should be playing outside are all turning boys off reading, new research suggests."

The problem with suggesting that teachers pick 'girls' books is probably thought to be solved by bringing more 'boys' books into the classroom. When actually the problem is that boys are socialised to reject or feel shame if they like things associated with girls. Now learning is the area for girls to succeed in, boys have got a real problem. So how about society stops shaming our boys? Then they'll read 'books'. It's very hard to be conscious of your own behaviour. Possibly overcompensating is a good thing here.

4th July 2012

The princess and taking the pee – our blog about stereotypes in children's books and a book list, and have promised a blog on films next month. We'll start compiling a film list in a similar style. So tell us the feminist kids' films you know.

People unsure if their suggestion is suitable. Don't worry, the film list will have to be a bit looser. Not many perfect feminist films out there! Whatever that would be.

(Part of Blog reprinted here)

The princess and taking the pee

We've been asked to write a monthly blog for Bea, and rather than simply expand on our diary entries, we decided to use it for something different. Recently someone wrote that most online articles on this subject only address the problem they are complaining about in the last paragraph. Big moan, small suggestion, down to the comments (oh the comments). We figure this would be a good rule to buck. So we're aiming to make this column as much about solutions as problems. We love a good moan as much as the next parent (we're so tired), but sometimes that can leave us feeling hopeless. So we're going to try to address some of the things that are making us furious. We're not talking about big changes, simply sharing the ways that we try to bring equality into our parenting. Also this is not a one way street, we want to hear your ideas too, because, as we've discovered on Twitter, together we're more powerful.

So what we'd like to do each month is to look at things like media, language, toys, films, sport and relationships, and deconstruct the problems and suggest alternatives. We're going to start with books. Here are the problems (and we're mostly talking about pre-school/primary books of the kind our kids have seen, but a lot of the problems are universal):

Male characters outweigh female characters significantly

Here's a study from the US on the skewed ratios of male to female characters in picture books,[8] which we can speculate gives children a view of the world that expects females to be less prominent but not just that, they also see…

Male characters partake in 'action', while female characters often do not

The original study mentioned above – Hamilton et al. (2006) noted, "Modern children's picture books continue to provide nightly reinforcement of the idea that boys and men are more interesting and important than are girls and women"

This is a bad situation for the psychology of girls AND for the attitude boys will have to girls and themselves.

Animals are most often referred to as 'he'

Seriously people, cows with udders are not male. It's one that most of us find very hard not to do. Most people will be brought up to automatically call an animal 'he'. Authors of kids' picture books are no exception. This compounds the problem of males being more important and females less visible.

The historical position of women is presented uncritically in fairy tales

Yeah, we're mostly talking princesses here. If you've never Jeff Brunner's deconstruction of Disney's upsettingly successful Princess brand, then read it, weep, and consider what message it's sending kids.[9]

No doubt you'll have some of your own favourites, but that'll do for now. So we'll suggest some books here that you can buy/take out the library which contradict the problems above.

You want action? Ladybird do a simple line of superhero phonics readers with titles including *Jumping Jade* and *Invisible Liz* by Mandy Ross.

Spot It! by Delphine Chedru is a simple but beautiful book where the reader has to find hidden animals – and some of them are female. Radical! If your kids love it, like ours do, you can get the sequel, *Spot It Again!*

In *The Paper Bag Princess* by Robert Munsch, a princess uses her wit to outsmart a dragon in order to rescue the prince. The prince, however isn't grateful enough to run off into the sunset with someone wearing a paper bag. She tells him "you are a bum" and they don't get married. The classic anti-princess book, but not strictly a traditional fairytale, so how about *Kate and the Beanstalk* by Mary Pope Osborne. Kate climbs the beanstalk, outwits the giant and brings home riches to her mother. Woot.

Finally, a book you can use to discuss the way the world divides us by our gender with your kids. *Horace And Morris But Mostly Dolores* by James Howe. The three characters are great friends until Horace and Morris become part of an exclusive boys' club and Dolores finds herself left out. Soon, she, too, finds her own club, where no boys are allowed and girls are supposed to have fun doing girl stuff. But after a while, Horace and Morris and Dolores realize they aren't happy at all doing what everyone in their clubs seem to enjoy. They miss each other. Is it too late to be friends again? Nah!

That's just a few ideas, but we've made a **reading list** which has loads more suggestions for the kind of books that show kids there's more than one way to live life and includes books up to age 14. Feel free to suggest more books for the list.

And if you like these books but they're not in your library suggest them to your librarian. This can really work, our council has an online form for making book suggestions.

You can also buy more books like this from Letterbox Library, a children's booksellers celebrating equality and diversity. Even better, suggest to a school that they should use Letterbox as a supplier.

Fill your house with the books you want your children to read and give them as presents to others. And for the books that your children choose without your input, edit books as you read aloud – say 'she' for every other animal. While they can't read, this is a temporary solution. When they are older discuss the problems you see with gender in books and encourage them to be critical of it.

Was that 50/50 moan and solution? There's nothing world changing here, but these are small ways you can show kids the kind of world you want to see.

Next month, Films – we'd love to hear your problems and suggestions for a film list in the comments below or on twitter @GenderDiary.

Diary continued

15th July 2012

Just remembered this from a while back. A relative with a boy aged 7 and a girl of 5 kept commenting on them pairing off with our 4-year-old and 1-year-old. The implication was that having gender in common was more significant than age in common. So though the boys had 6 years between them, they would still prefer each other's company to that of the girls. I didn't notice the kids had this preference. Although the adult would use language and divide them by their games, "Do you girls want to do...?" Etc. Adults can presume your interests and who you want to play with.

@brilliantfreak: What's more, the language implies to the children that they should prefer to play together than with the opposite sex

@GenderDiary: If you could pop that in a memo to the rest of the population too, that'd be great

21th July 2012

Interesting chat on girls in sport with Tanni Grey-Thompson (@Tanni_GT) on BBC Radio 4 Saturday Live. She says mothers are more likely to take sons to sport than daughters.

A twitter discussion on this between Tanni Grey Thompson and Carrie Dunn (writer and academic), went as follows:

Carrie: My PhD research covers this a bit. Depends on mother's attitude to sport, order of children and the sport itself as well as the club/venue chosen.

GenderDiary: An expert on tap, brilliant! So tell us, are mothers more likely to take kids to sports classes than fathers?

Tanni: Think dads are more likely to take them.

GenderDiary: If more dads take kids to sport do they take boys and girls equally? Is it just mothers who show bias? I'd be amazed if fathers showed no bias.

Carrie: My work is on attending sport. Done a bit on participation, and depending on sport, yes, mums don't want girls to be 'abnormal' or 'unfeminine' so don't encourage it.

Tanni: It's hard for mums. Girls doing sport are portrayed as not feminine / different.

Carrie: Absolutely. And a lot of factors create that feeling.

Tanni: Not an easy solution either. If it was we would have done it.

Carrie: Not just sport that's the problem!

GenderDiary: Thanks to you both for explaining. Very interesting.

24th July 2012

This just in from the kids' aunt: "Sitting by pool with 2-year-old on my knee looking at *Where's Wally?* book, finding the characters amongst the pyramids. The girl on her mummy's knee next to us was showing interest and her mum told her it was a boy's book! Wtf?! I said I didn't think it was a boy's book, and that my daughter loves it just as much as her brothers."

Our son was pointing to dirt on his t-shirt today and the childminder told him, "It's ok, mummy will wash it". Er, dad does the washing in this house!

I was reading something earlier worth sharing: Head of Podiatry Services at an Oxfordshire Community Health NHS Trust, Philip Joyce said, "High heels have a long history of social status, sexuality and power. It is not really surprising, by the time girls are 4-years-old they know that Disney's high-heeled glass slipper does not fit the ugly women".

27th July 2012

Oh Germany. Pink outfits for the women, blue for the men. It's bad enough for kids. Didn't you see those suffragettes earlier? #London2012

2nd August 2012

It's this femininity issue that stops girls doing sport. Olympic weightlifter Zoe Smith's response tells it like it is; *Olympic Weightlifter Responds To Sexist Tweets: 'We Don't Lift Weights...For The Likes Of Men Like That'* (Think Progress, 31st July 2012). The article says, "While Smith was preparing to set an Olympic record for Great Britain in the clean-and-jerk event, men (and some women) on Twitter were busy saying she wasn't attractive enough, or that she was manly, or that there was something wrong with her body because she was so muscular."

Here come the Olympic femininity police – writing in mainstream newspapers, putting young girls off sport. Unbelievable, *Women's judo: it's disturbing to watch these girls beat each other up* (Daily Telegraph, 2nd August 2012). Also, the BBC3 presenter earlier did his own bit of femininity-policing when he was shocked that Gemma Gibbons hadn't washed her hair today. Seriously though. That Telegraph piece is a hackers joke, yeah? Telegraph online using Daily Mail as a template. I know we're just driving traffic their way. Ug. I'm sure, not many youngsters are reading the Telegraph! But if parents are put off then kids are put off by them.

4th August 2012

Women's football Team GB went out last night, sadly. But obviously lots of other great teams still to watch. Taking our 4-year-old to Wembley on Monday! Really impressed by the intelligence, confidence and humour of teenage athletes Zoe Smith and Katarina Johnson-Thompson. Ace role models.

A classic. At a children's party entertainers give out stickers at the end – princesses for girls, dinosaurs for boys. Consequently at bedtime our daughter is arranging all her stickers according to what's for girls and what's for boys. Had to have a chat explaining no-one can dictate what you can like.

At the same party the entertainers make much humour from how horrible/scary a (fake) worm is. Our daughter used to pick up worms happily, but recently won't. Also interestingly entertainers make a thing of the 'threat' of male half kissing one of the girls because "girls don't want kisses from boys". Now, I don't really want either of my children kissing others willy nilly, I want them to exercise discretion. However I also don't want them thinking kissing is weird or undesirable. One of the ways boys and girls are separated from young age.

11th August 2012

Just writing up the film list for kids. Any more suggestions for films that don't stick to the usual gender stereotypes gratefully received. The list will be up on Tuesday, will tweet links.

12th August 2012

4-year-old earlier, "Boys look 'smart' in clothes and girls look 'pretty'." Well yes most people do use those words. Hard to argue against.

14th August 2012

Our blog this month, on inequality in kids' films, and our list of great films that buck that trend.

Any more suggestions for the list? Know any kids' films with lead male characters who break stereotypes?

(Blog reprinted here)

A league of their own

We love films. Before we had kids we used to have a weekly cinema club, a bit like a book club. We'd go with the same group of friends every Monday night and then discuss the film afterwards over a cheap dinner. Back then though, I don't think we were aware of the Bechdel test. If you've been living under a rock you won't know that it's a depressingly spare way of fathoming whether a film has a female presence in it with these 3 checks:

1. It includes at least two women,

2. who have at least one conversation,

3. about something other than a man or men

Alison Bechdel brought the idea to the world with an awesome comic strip explanation of how it works. I'm pretty certain that our weekly club would have been monthly at best if the films always had to pass Bechdel.

Those who haven't heard of the Bechdel test may well want to plead that it's ridiculous and that most films have women in them. We're so used to the reality of the media that we've been brought up with that sometimes it's hard to see what's going on in front of our noses. Bechdeltest.com lists films by whether they pass the test. Here's the bad news. You think of most major children's films in recent years and they'll usually struggle to pass the test – Shrek, Toy Story and Ice Age and all their sequels, for example, don't pass. Seriously, this is not on.

The Geena Davis Institute on Gender in the Media (yes *that* Geena Davis), who are conducting research and consciousness raising on the issue, will tell you this:

Males outnumber females 3 to 1 in family films. In contrast, females comprise just over 50% of the population in the United States. Even more staggering is the fact that this ratio, as seen in family films, is the same as it was in 1946.

Females are almost four times as likely as males to be shown in sexy attire. Further, females are nearly twice as likely as males to be shown with a diminutive waistline. Generally unrealistic figures are more likely to be seen on females than males.

Females are also underrepresented behind the camera. Across 1,565 content creators, only 7% of directors, 13% of writers, and 20% of producers are female. This translates to 4.8 males working behind-the-scenes to every one female.

From 2006 to 2009, not one female character was depicted in G-rated family films in the field of medical science, as a business leader, in law, or politics. In these films, 80.5% of all working characters are male and 19.5% are female, which is a contrast to real world statistics, where women comprise 50% of the workforce.

We're in the UK, and obviously these stats are for the USA, but realistically the majority of big screen films our kids see at the cinema come from the USA. Unlike our previous blog about books and the conservative nature of the publishing industry, the stakes are so much higher in film because of the cost of production. Not that that's any excuse!

So here we go, that was the moaning section, now here's some alternatives to the non-representative dross. Here's some great kids films that have females in abundance and also pass Bechdel.

My Neighbour Totoro (1988). Where would 21st century children be without Studio Ghibli? When two sisters move to the country to be near their ailing mother, they have adventures with the wonderous forest spirits who live nearby. Ghibli has managed to produce films that have complex and interesting characters of both genders for years now. Look over there Hollywood, it ain't *that* hard!

Labyrinth (1986) was an important film for many of us growing up. It's only now looking back that you might realise the feminist message. Remember that important line that releases Sarah from the grip of Jareth, "You have no power over me." That's an important message for a teenage girl. Still relevant.

Spirited Away (2001) is an Alice in Wonderland-style tale which sees Chihiro and her family wander into a world ruled by gods, witches, and monsters. Complex, layered and imaginative – not things often said about kids' films.

Whale Rider (2002) deals with the pain and rejection that a traditional patriarchal culture can bring. A young Maori girl fights to fulfill a destiny her grandfather refuses to recognize. Powerful and beautiful.

Finally, want to reinforce a bit of that Olympics feel good factor that has hopefully inspired girls to get out there and try sports? Well *Fast Girls* (2012) focuses on training hard to achieve a goal, while also being touching and funny. The actresses trained alongside Team GB athletes to prepare for the roles, which makes it even more ace.

So we never put Bechdel into practice in our cinema-going days, but frankly it's not exactly possible to do the test before you've seen the film. We've actually invented our own kids' version of Bechdel. It's also incredibly simple: Every other film we go to see has to have a female lead. (There's a big prize for someone who comes up with a catchy name for our test, I can't think of one). No doubt you can guess that this is also going to keep you out of the cinema. It's do-able with young kids like ours but is unlikely to be possible when they're older. But so far we've only broken our rule once, and that was because of the relentless rain over the winter

(*Happy Feet Two* was very much not worth breaking it for though, let me tell you).

The principle of staying away from the cinema means you're voting with your feet and your wallet. If people go in droves to see new assertive, female-led films like *Brave*, then hopefully we'll send the industry a message.

So there are some thoughts and a few gems of films, but there are many more on our longer film list. I'm sure you can think of some more, so tweet us. Sadly, unlike our book list, finding films that show an alternative to the male stereotype have not sprung to mind. Please let us know if you think of any, we'd like to add them to the list.

Next month, sport.

(List reprinted here)

Film list for kids age 0-14

This is a crowd-sourced list of films, so we haven't seen them all, but they've been recommended as having themes that are broadly feminist. It will go without saying that there are never any 'perfect' films, although it's nice to know they should all pass the Bechdel Test and then some, and are marked as such. We hope it's helpful.

If you'd like to suggest films to add to the list then tweet us @GenderDiary

Cetificate U (Suitable for all)

Lilo & Stitch (2002) Passes Bechdel

Orphaned Hawaiian girl Lilo lives with her 19-year-old sister, Nani. The two girls have been struggling to make it on their own. A no-nonsense social worker tells Nani she has three days to prove she's an appropriate guardian. Meanwhile, Stitch, a mischief-making alien, has escaped from the planet Turo. Stitch is adopted by Lilo and leaves a wide path of chaos in his wake.

My Neighbour Totoro (1988) Not Bechdel listed

Where would 21st century children be without studio Ghibli? When two sisters move to the country to be near their ailing mother, they have adventures with the wonderous forest spirits who live nearby. Ghibli magic.

Hoodwinked! (2005) Passes Bechdel

Hoodwinked fuses the classic fairy tale of *Little Red Riding Hood* with the criss-crossing storylines of film noir – pretty ambitious stuff for a computer-animated cartoon. Well known fairy tale given a twist.

The Secret Garden (1993) Passes Bechdel

Opening in India in the early 1900s, when Mary is orphaned she is sent to live in Misselthwaite Manor with her melancholy uncle who is often away. Mary explores the estate alone until she finds friends. Together they restore a neglected garden. Mary is ace. And Maggie Smith is in it.

Matilda (1996) Passes Bechdel

Neglected by her stupid, self-interested parents, the remarkably intelligent Matilda develops telekinetic powers. The original book is on our booklist, and though the film is not as good as the book, it's worth a mention because the main character is a strong, confident and brilliant girl.

The Hideaways (1973) Not Bechdel listed

A young brother and sister run away from home and hide out in the Metropolitan Museum of Art. The girl becomes entranced with a statue that has baffled experts. She becomes determined to track down its former owner and uncover the secrets for herself. Based on the children's book *From the mixed-up files of Mrs Basil E. Frankweiler.*

Mary Poppins (1964) Passes Bechdel

Gotta love the IMDB summary of this: "A magic nanny comes to work for a cold banker's unhappy family." Well yes, but also a 60s critique of patriarchy and capitalism. Mary Poppins is in control of everything and entirely independent. And it's got suffragettes.

The Railway Children (1970) Not Bechdel listed

The Waterbury's happy middle-class Edwardian life is shattered when their father leaves one night without explanation. Their mother takes the children to the countryside where she earns money through writing. The children become fascinated with the railway line. I can break into tears just thinking about the ending. But that's not the point here. Bobby is clever and kind and spunky and it's a brilliant story about how children can be powerful in their own right.

The Rescuers (1974) Passes Bechdel

Two mice of the Rescue Aid Society search for a little girl kidnapped by unscrupulous treasure hunters. Though this shows its age now (there are some sexist comments that irritate me on every viewing in our house), it is unusual in having several main female characters of varying and interesting sorts – all of them are brave and forthright, including the baddie.

Labyrinth (1986) Passes Bechdel

15-year-old Sarah accidentally wishes her baby half-brother away to the Goblin King, Jareth, who will keep him if Sarah does not complete his Labyrinth in 13 hours. Remember that important line, "You have no power over me." That's an important message for a teenage girl.

Kiki's Delivery Service (1989) Passes Bechdel

A young witch, on her mandatory year of independent life, finds fitting into a new community difficult while she supports herself by running an air courier service.

The Wild Thornberrys (2002) Not Bechdel listed

Eliza and Debbie are two sisters who don't always get along. But their relationship is put to the test when Debbie's life is in danger, and Eliza might have to give up her power to talk to animals.

Certificate PG (Parental Guidance)

Enchanted (2007) Passes Bechdel

An archetypal Disney Princess is dropped in the middle of modern day New York. Soon after her arrival, Princess Giselle begins to change her views on life and love. Recommended by a follower because it's "good at breaking stereotypes, challenges roles and she becomes self-employed!"

Castle in the Sky (1986) Not Bechdel listed

Inspired by Gulliver's Travels, the orphan Sheeta, with the help of Pazu and a rollicking band of sky pirates, makes her way to the ruins of the once great sky-kingdom of Laputa. Sheeta and Pazu must outwit the evil Muska.

Spirited Away (2001) Passes Bechdel

An Alice in Wonderland style tale which sees Chihiro and her family wander into a world ruled by gods, witches, and monsters. When her parents are changed into pigs Chihiro flees. She befriends a boy, and learns the rules of the land. Complex, layered and imaginative – not things often said about kids' films.

Nausicaä of the Valley of the Wind (1984) Not Bechdel listed

It's a thousand years since the war that almost wiped out the whole of the human race. A ship crashes in the valley and warrior/pacifist Princess Nausicaä desperately struggles to prevent two warring nations from destroying themselves and their dying planet. Described in one review as "the only princess story worth watching." She basically protects the whole planet.

MirrorMask (2005) Passes Bechdel

In a fantasy world of opposing kingdoms, a 15-year-old girl must find the fabled MirrorMask in order to save the kingdom and get home. This is not only a movie that passes the Bechdel test with flying colors, it's a film with a resourceful, intelligent, and most of all believable young woman as a main character who overcomes long odds with her intellect and creativity.

Ever After: A Cinderella Story (1998) Passes Bechdel

The "real" story of Cinderella. A refreshing take on the classic fairy tale – so says the blurb. Slightly sceptical about this one, but we haven't seen it, so feel free to tell us otherwise.

Brave (2012) Passes Bechdel

Determined to make her own path in life, Princess Merida defies a custom that brings chaos to her kingdom. Granted one wish, Merida must rely on her bravery and her archery skills to undo a beastly curse.

Bridge to Terabithia (2007) Passes Bechdel

A preteen's life is changed after befriending the new girl at school. We've already plot-spoiled this over on our book list, so we'll leave the summary at that. Haven't seen this film version but expect it to be thoughtful, sad and moving like the novel.

Whale Rider (2002) Passes Bechdel

A contemporary story of love, rejection and triumph as a young Maori girl fights to fulfil a destiny her grandfather refuses to recognize. A film that deals with the pain that a traditional patriarchal culture can bring into the life of a young girl. Powerful and beautiful.

Certificate 12A (Suitable for 12 years and over)

Fast Girls (2012) Passes Bechdel

Shania and Lisa come from different backgrounds but both want to qualify for a major world athletics championship. The actresses trained alongside Team GB athletes to prepare for the roles. The film focuses on training hard to achieve a goal, which is nice. It's also funny, touching and action packed.

The Hunger Games (2012) Passes Bechdel

16-year-old Katniss Everdeen volunteers to take the place of her sister in the yearly Hunger Games where underprivileged youth fight to the death to entertain the rich and give hope to the poor – but not too much. In the ruins of North America she must go up against Tributes who have trained for the Games all their lives. Only one contestant can win.

Diary continued

19th August 2012

Off on holiday.

8th September 2012

An early morning gender based encounter. Me (mum) and 22-month-old spend a lovely 20 minutes in an empty sun dappled playground. Then lots of men with toddlers start arriving. One tells his kid to watch out for "that little girl" then says, "Boy. Sorry is he a boy?" I say yes and it doesn't matter. He tells me his daughter is very tough and everyone thinks she's a boy, and they dress her in blue to confuse people. Then he asks why I'm there because Saturday morning is the dad's job. I tell him dad is at the 4-year-old's swimming lesson and this is the easy job compared to doing the hair wash. An interesting melting pot of gender and gender roles in the playground this morning.

10th September 2012

I'm pretty sure starting school is going to be a rich source of material for this diary. Got some things to share when I have a free moment. Boys who haven't been socialised to dislike pink/'girls' things' before school often seem to change their views once they start.

12th September 2012

I find myself conflicted between promoting strong female role models and not being dismissive of 'girly' things. Complex thing. It can be a tricky path to tread between embracing 'feminine' things and heading down a path of traditional gender roles. It's often hard not to tie yourself up into feminist knots.

MT @hugoschwyzer: *Feminist fathers, feminist sons: A Conversation with Michael and Zachary Kimmel* (RoleReboot, 12th September 2012)

Nice quote from last RT that sums up our feeling: "*Friends and family, knowing our views and what we do for a living, repeatedly told us both that "you'll see that biology really is destiny". Kimmel noted that people tend to presume expertise resting solely on their own experience, issuing sweeping generalizations about gender roles based on a sample size of one or two.*"

Doing an Usborne 'Sticker dressing Romans' book with the 4-year-old yesterday she said, "Why are there no women's clothes in this book?" Good question.

MT @day_jess: Sent [a letter] to Usborne in June, [saying] my 5-year-old has written twice to ask why there are no girls in 'Sticker dressing long ago' Why no reply? "Do they think there weren't any girls in history?" she asked. Got an email after the tweet. I had to reply to the email and ask them if they could write to my daughter, who had written to them twice in the first place.

GenderDiary: Did their letter to a 5-year-old say 'it's a book for boys and boys don't want to see any girls in their books'?

RT @day_jess: Essentially, yes, hedged about a bit. And they sent her 'Kings and Queens' as that has women in.

It's depressing that our society accepts it's OK that boys don't want/shouldn't like females in their books. Change this people! Don't tell me boys just won't read books with girls in. Our culture shames boys for liking anything 'female'. Perpetuating it doesn't help.

On a positive note, this book she chose at the library today, *Miranda the Castaway* by James Mayhew, is great. About

a girl using survival skills on an island. Miranda builds a
system that transports water, through pipes, to her tree
house. I think adults often fail to recognise that their
influence pushes boys away from female characters.

14th September 2012

The Paralympics/Olympics were great eh? But girls in the
UK are worryingly inactive. Our blog on gender and sport.

(Blog reprinted here)

I can't tonight, I'm washing my hair

When we went to an open day at our daughter's new school, the teacher giving us the tour told us what after school clubs were available. Girls' football was one of them, and obviously we *had* to ask, why isn't it a mixed club? The teacher said it's because the girls feel more confident playing this way. And who can blame them? As Professor Carrie Petcher said to one of us recently (feminist name drop, boom!), "the boys won't pass to the girls". I guess it's hard to see yourself as a star striker when half your team are undermining your efforts.

In the warm glow of the Olympic and Paralymic success story, it's easy to imagine that sport is now on the top of every child's hobby list. But there are ongoing sexist issues that explain this:

Just 12% of 14-year-old girls in the UK are reaching the recommended levels of physical activity – half the number of boys at the same age.[10]

Shocking stuff. The excellent piece of **research** that brings us this awful statistic uncovered a wealth of interesting information. It found, for example, that boys and girls both agree that there are more opportunities for boys to do sport than girls, and also that girls' experience of sport at school can really put them off it. But here's when it really gets down to the nitty gritty:

Half of the girls surveyed (48%) say that getting sweaty is "not feminine."

Nearly a third of boys think that girls who are sporty are not very feminine.

Aha! Woop woop, it's the sound of the gender police.

Sport is not feminine, where on earth would anyone get such an idea?? Oh, er, just everywhere. When Gemma Gibbons won Team GB's first judo medal in 12 years, did she get the admiration of every man, woman and child in the country. No, she got a poisonous blog in The Daily Telegraph asking if "women fighting each other violently is a perfectly wholesome spectator sport?"[11] Now the Telegraph has clearly set itself on a new economic strategy along the lines of the Daily Mail, but the way these papers do that is by writing something that appeals to people's basest prejudices and that they'd like to have confirmed. GIRLS, FIGHTING, TOGETHER?! IT'S THE END OF DAYS! No, thimble-brain, it's sport. Get a grip.

Later, the male presenter on the BBC also policed the femininity of the judo medallist when she revealed she hadn't washed her hair that day. Shocked, he was. Oh piss off, say we. But that's the problem summed up in one small exchange on television. A woman can win an Olympic medal, the pinnacle of her career, and a man can take the time to be appalled that she didn't groom her hair to his expectations. This tells girls that maintaining their appearance trumps the achievements of physical activity. And that's very much what this report found. Being sporty made a boy one of the most popular among his peers. I think you can guess that the same was not true for girls.

Here's another finding:

Boys were commonly cited by girls of all ages as a reason for why sport and physical activity is not perceived to be fun, particularly in relation to school PE lessons. Boys' negative attitudes about girls' abilities in sport and physical activity were also perceived to be a problem.

The attitudes of the other half of the population are a big factor in why girls shun sport.

So remember our policy, a bit of a moan and then some ideas for solutions. Well this isn't as straight forward as a list of books with girls in. But there really are things you can do.

The Women's Sport and Fitness Foundation, who compiled that research has been trying to make us all wake up to the growing problem of inactivity in girls. Their #gogirl campaign strap line, "Our vision is a society which encourages, enables and celebrates active women and girls." Well yes that's nice, how do we do that? Well guess what, parents? To add to the multitude of responsibilities that are on your shoulders, you are a big influence here. Taking children to watch or participate in sport is vital. Not just talking about it, going out and doing it. You're also a role model for them in terms of whether you are participating in sport.

The marvellous Carrie Dunn is doing a PhD on this very subject. Her feeling is that access to watch sport needs to be the starting focus. Girls are less likely to be taken to sport than boys. Parents are equally likely to fall into the trap of policing their daughter's femininity by being less encouraging about sport for girls. Carrie's research has found that if girls are encouraged to think that they are allowed to watch whatever sport they want, then they will. Simples, eh? If it's presented to them as a gendered choice, i.e only for their brothers, then they're likely to see sport as gendered for the rest of their lives.

We've been unbelievably lucky to have the Olympics on our doorstep at a time when our daughter is just old enough to be able to enjoy and understand how exciting sport can be to watch. She saw table tennis, basketball, football, athletics and the modern pentathlon, with disabled and able-bodied athletes competing. We hope it's something that will stay with her for the rest of her life. But will it make her more likely to take part in sport?

Carrie wrote that despite growing up with great role models like Sally Gunell and Liz McColgan, she still hated sport at school.[12] It's true, sports role models don't necessarily have the effect of changing our physical behaviour. But here's where we hope that their power to influence can work in other ways.

Athletes like Zoe Smith, Nicola Adams, Katarina Johnson-Thompson and Laura Robson, are smart, witty, confident and incredibly good at standing up to a world that has ridiculous expectations of them because they are women. Zoe Smith wrote the most fantastic blog post in response to tweets criticising her appearance as 'manly'. She wrote,

"What makes you think we actually give a toss that you, personally, do not find us attractive? ...We, as any women with an ounce of self-confidence would, prefer our men to be confident enough in themselves to not feel emasculated by the fact that we aren't weak and feeble."[13]

So though our girls may not look at these young women and be galvanised to become champion pole vaulters, what I hope they will take on board is seeing high profile women who are refusing to suffer under the pressure of our appearance driven culture, because that's a big part of what is holding girls back. Young role models like these have been pretty lacking. As adults, we find them incredibly inspiring.

Raising the profile of women's sport can only help to dispel prejudices about ability and importance. So get signing the current petition asking the Government to discuss the state of women's sport in the House of Commons and to consider making broadcasters obligated to show women's sport.

But the most important point in the area of raising the profile, audiences and television coverage of women's sport? Take your sons to watch it, because it's their attitudes that are part of this problem.

Diary continued

27th September 2012

Still shocked by the Rochdale girl's account of police failing to investigate her abuse on BBC Radio 4 *Today* programme earlier. It's on *Woman's Hour* at greater length now. So appalling. Worst part is that police told her parents it was a "lifestyle choice" and they wouldn't do anything because she was six months from being 16.[14]

3rd October 2012

We keep telling each other about diary things we need to tweet but don't seem to find the time. As they get older it gets more complex too.

4th October 2012

Ah, school.
4-year-old: I wish I was still at nursery with [names 2 boys] so we can play car races.

Me: You can play races with kids at your school.

4-year-old: Not with girls.

Me: (Long explanation of why all games are for all children).

4-year-old: I wanted to play with the boys but they said I can't. But that's not fair because the class rules say always let others play your games.

On this subject. I was talking to a friend who was worried her daughter starting school would have trouble fitting in with the other girls. It reminded me that it is totally assumed that children's friends will be from their own gender only. It's just a given.

One from a while ago I had meant to tweet. At the circus. A gran and her granddaughter and grandson on the row in front. Granddaughter is age 9ish, and told, "Pull your skirt down and put your legs together." I wondered to myself why we insist on dressing girls in clothes that actually just expose parts of their bodies that we insist they be modest about and ashamed of. Crackers isn't it?!

9th October 2012

14 year-old Pakistani activist who championed education for girls has been shot in the head by a Taliban gunman.[15]

I'm at #demoswomen event at Tory conference. Not really addressing early years element of austerity etc. that we care about.

Oops. Both of us tweeting tonight but in different places. I got confused there for a while.

Another spot.Standing in a shopping centre with the 6-year-old looking at a notice board. Two large adverts, one for a dancing school with a girl in a tutu, one for Socatots with a cartoon boy playing football on it. Gender cues are picked up from as young as 18 moths. It doesn't need the word 'boy' or 'girl' on the advert, sadly.

10th October 2012

Survey by Girl Guides reveals that marriage is not the key definition of success. These co-habitors agree.

11th October 2012

An exciting meeting of minds tonight as @GenderDiary go to the pub with @PinkStinksUK. Expect the world to be put to rights by 9:15pm.

14th October 2012

Our blog about ways to get kids in school to understand
sexism:

(Blog reprinted here)

Never too young to learn

Ah school, the best days of your life. Our 4-year-old has just started school. Here's a typical conversation when she gets picked up at the end of the day:

Parent: What did you learn today at school, darling?

4-year-old: Oh you know, just the usual reinforcing of traditional gender roles through a complex combination of adults' different treatment of children depending on their gender, and peers who police my behaviour to make sure I don't break out of stereotypical behaviour, and that. Oh, and we did some clay modelling and I made a snail.

Parent: Great, did you remember to bring your PE kit home?

Yes, for the gender-concerned parent, school is the final frontier in exposing your child to the world as it really is. We've heard many, many times from followers whose kids did not conform or particularly take note of the 'things that are for girls' and the 'things that are for boys' until they went to school. The most typical is the boy who likes pink. Several of our kids' male cousins loved pink until school had the mean-heartedness to wring it out of them. It also tugged on the heart strings the other day when the 4-year-old said she wanted to go back to nursery where she could play car races with the boys there, because the boys at school won't let her play their games. (And before you ask, of course she was reminded that girls play cars too).

There are so many reasons why school can be fuel for the fire of gender divisions. As the 4-year-old so cleverly pointed out, research shows that teaching staff do treat boys and girls differently. In a 2006 UK research paper of children aged 7-8 and their teachers, they found, "Whilst the pupils believed

143

their teachers treated them in a fair and just manner, three quarters of the teachers interviewed believed they did or should respond differently to pupils according to gender."[16]

And to those that think it's necessary because girls and boys (yes all of them, because every single girl is the same as every single other girl, yah?) learn in different ways, read the conclusions of that paper.

So what's to do? Well overthrow the patriarchy first and foremost, obv, but if that doesn't come off before half term, here's our suggestions for ways you can get some badly needed lessons about sexism into a school near you.

A blog post by the excellent @bluemilk describes her experience of running an anti-sexism session in her daughter's school class of 5 and 6-year-olds.[17] She's not a teacher but was asked if she'd be interested in doing it. Our daughter's school has similarly asked parents if they'd like to present anything to classes that they have a particular interest in. If you get the same opportunity in your kids' schools then grab it with both hands. @bluemilk describes a brilliant set of photos and questions she used to challenge the kids' assumptions about gender, for example:

"The kids were really receptive and by the conclusion of the workshop were readily able to spot sexism in toy catalogues presented to them and were happily repeating phrases in their analysis that I'd been using throughout the workshop, like "colours are for everyone", "feelings are for everyone" and "toys are for everyone".

Do read it and even if you don't do something as big as a workshop, it will give you lots of great ideas for things to say to kids when you want to challenge something they say that is sexist.

Ditto this piece, *It's Okay to be Neither* by Melissa Bollow Tempel, a teacher who had a kid in her class who presented with gender variance.[18] She similarly worked on sessions that used photos and questions to challenge assumptions and is well worth plundering ideas from.

A more formal way of getting this stuff into your kid's school could be Laura Nelson's Breakthrough Gender Stereotypes Project which has completed an initial trial in a school with 9 and 10-year-olds, holding two weeks of gender stereotypes awareness lessons and includes elements of science, geography, history, politics and sociology. The website says, "If you work in a school, or indeed if you work with children who you think would benefit from these lessons, we would love to hear from you."

Finally, the Astell Project is "a campaign and community of activists and educators which aims to get Women and Gender Studies introduced into schools for 13 to 15-year-old girls and boys." Which is an ambitious aim in the current education climate. You can help them by signing their petition.

Now in previous blogs we've usually had a resource for you to draw on, and we'd like to have a template for something similar to the parent-led workshops mentioned above, but the dog ate it. Hopefully we'll get that handed in to you in the coming weeks, but in the meantime, as usual, any ideas you can share with us to add to this resource would be gratefully received. Our previous experiences of compiling lists and so on, is that we're stronger when we put our heads together to use our collective wisdom. Yes, some of you guys clearly picked up a lot in school, but what you managed to shake off was the idea that your gender defined the things you would think. How clever of you! But we all know it's not that easy. So let's try and give our kids the head start that we never had.

Diary continued

15th October 2012

Check out the name of these shoes @day_jess spotted: Girls Bootleg Shoes by Clarks called "No Playing". Sad.

19th October 2012

This issue of boys being shamed for doing/liking 'girl' things preoccupies me a lot. It lays the foundations of misogyny and homophobia. We need a sort of Pink Stinks for boys. Macho Stinks or something (!). I'm thinking aloud.

At the library earlier. Trying out piles of books always highlights repetitive narratives – mums are ever-present carers and Dads missing. #Yawn

23rd October 2012

Got a call from school today to say our daughter had walked into a tree. Nice work. Told a relative on the phone later, she explained that girls often get cuts and scrapes because they're too busy chatting. Boys of course get injured 'being boys'. She's saying boys injure themselves doing things, same injuries to girls explained as happening to them. Passive.

27th October 2012

Ug. Advert for kids' build it yourself JCB digger, with a deep voiced man shouting, "TOUGH TOYS, FOR TOUGH BOYS." Just like 'men's' adverts.

Excited about book 'The Gender Trap' by Dr. Emily Kane, hoping it sums up what we feel.

1st November 2012

Our daughter has an odd way of putting her coat on — upside down then flips it over her head. Her childminder says it's how a boy would put coat on.

5th November 2012

I [GenderDiary mum] was a tomboy, and was proud of it. But I think I internalised the way boys are taught to look down on girl things.

7th November 2012

Who was it that was furious about the Gruffalo being marketed to boys only in Sainsbury's? John Lewis are too under the sign 'slippers for boys'.

Also in John Lewis — Two steps forward one step back: football boots in a rainbow of colours but only in the boys section.

12th November 2012

Interesting thing — we've never been trolled. I often think it's because they don't know which person they're addressing. But anonymity hasn't stopped some people being bullied — and indeed — outed. So it's not necessarily a secure barrier. I think trolling can be very gender based, particularly for anti-feminists. So they may not know your name but they know you're a woman. But with us, they don't. And my guess is that this throws them a curveball.

13th November 2012

Flexible working announcement [from the government] today. Statement from the Fatherhood Institute on why it won't work, signed by Rebecca Asher and more.

Girlguiding UK latest research:

11% of boys think it can be ok to hit their partner for talking to someone else at a party.

85% of girls think childcare should be shared equally between parents.

68% of girls believe women are judged more on appearance than ability.

12% of boys say it's ok to pressure their partner to have sex, 3% of girls agree.

Check out @NewToFeminism – who founded the #TwitterYouthFeministArmy getting discussions going with younger #feminists – fab!

Hasbro: Star Wars website, looking for Xmas present for daughter. Choose by 'Gender' button is more annoying than usual.

14th November 2012

Helped @Bristol_Jane find a present from our reading list. Keep it in mind for Christmas.

Had an interesting diary entry this weekend, but it was too big to tweet, so it's in this blog about language and kids:

(Blog reprinted here)

Are you a people person?

"For me, words are a form of action, capable of influencing change. Their articulation represents a complete, lived experience"

                                                                    Ingrid Bengis

Words. Dontcha just love 'em? But sometimes the 140 characters of twitter are just too short to record things that happen to our kids because of their gender. Here's a slightly longer story that happened at the weekend that really sums up why we keep a diary about these things.

We were visiting the playground of an aeroplane museum with the children's cousins. Five kids, aged 5-2. Two girls, three boys.

Things that were said by an adult with us:

About a remote controlled aeroplane, "Look at the aeroplane doing stunts, he's obviously having a wonderful time. Look at him go. He's really enjoying himself."

To oldest boy child, by name, specifically "Can you see the engines in there, behind the propellers? That's what makes the plane fly. Can you see all the parts inside?"

To everyone, about the volunteers who run the museum "Men love this stuff don't they? They have such a good time here."

Later at home our daughter tells her cousin she wants a remote control aeroplane for Christmas. He tells her that girls can't have them and only dolls and Barbies are for girls. Also, he tells her, he hates dolls and Barbies.

D'ya see a pattern here at all. Well do ya? How confusing the world must have been for these kids at the end of the day, when their parents tried to explain to them why *all* toys are for *everyone*!

Yes, the language we use shapes the way children understand the world. Language, among other things, tells kids what roles people of their gender will fulfil when they are older. They can try to kick against it, but there's often someone there to tell them they're wrong about wanting to break those boundaries.

Let's look at that first example of language where someone uses 'he' to describe the gender of someone (or something, an aeroplane in this case) even though they don't know the gender of that person/thing. In Brian D Earp's recent article from the *Journal of Communication and Culture* on so-called he/man generics, he explains why it's damaging:

"This has the effect of minimizing women's importance and diverting attention away from their very existence. The result is a sort of invisibility – in the language itself, in the individual's mind's eye, and in the broader social consciousness."[9]

As always @GenderDiary, is here to bring you good news. Earp's research shows that use of the masculine generic pronoun in English has fallen dramatically in recent years, while non-sexist alternatives have gradually taken their place.

Earp recorded a marked decline in the use of the term "mankind", while "humankind," on the other hand, saw a 1890% increase (from 63 articles in 1970-1971 to 1192 articles in 1999-2000). "He or she," (rather than just using "he") for its part, saw a 1194% increase. It's gratifying that this is already happening. But you can help it along too.

You won't be surprised that we'd encourage you to use gender-neutral language with kids when you can. In our house, we are not remotely militant about it, but, boy, girl,

150

man, woman, him, her etc. are less likely to be heard than kids, children, people, person, them and they.

Those who want to accuse us of terrible political correctness are very welcome to do it, but they'll find that they're fighting against a trend in language that is happening anyway. By releasing as many parts of language as possible from the limits of gender, you allow children to choose for themselves whether something is relevant to them. The conversations that we had on that outing sent our children clear messages that gender was relevant to what we were seeing. Boys and men like aeroplanes, is the message they got. The message we got is that by using more neutral language we're helping to keep options open for our kids, and our daughter will be getting a remote control aeroplane for Christmas.

Diary continued

15th November 2012

Goldieblox (a construction toy for girls) is what I call the appeasement approach. It makes me feel uncomfortable, though I see the need. Summary: It's easy to feel the likelihood of smashing learned gender roles is impossible so this type of appeasement is useful. Discuss.

I find it hard to compromise on my position that I want to treat children as individuals, not manifestations of their gender. But I also understand that some people live in the real world. My grey area is whether the product helps children whose families are not touched by feminism at all? Appeasement is not my position. But I have an understanding of why some people think it's ok.

Hasbro has only five women in Guess Who? but they don't understand why a 6-year-old girl objects. Wake up dinosaurs! (*Guess Who's sexist? Classic board game's gender bias leaves six-year-old fuming*, Independent 17 Nov 2012).

16th November 2012

The ace Geena Davis Institute on Gender in Media have released a short clip about how girls are affected by their representation.

19th November 2012

A girl's 6th birthday party at the weekend. 12 girls were invited. That's weird right? When I was that age I had playdates and parties with boys and girls. The thing is, my folks' had an unreconstructed 1950s gender outlook, but it was normal to them that I play with both (when young at least). Has something changed? Six seems really young to be segregating from opposite gender.

Which reminds me. I found this nice book in the library about a boy who wants to be an angel in the school Nativity, *Alfie's Angels* by Henriette Barkow.

20th November 2012

I see Hasbro's replied again to @jenoconnell's 6-year-old about Guess Who? having only 5 female characters.[20]

28th November 2012

Hello to new follower @LetToysBeToys who I'm sure lots of our followers will be interested in.

29th November 2012

RT @MentalHealthCop: I hate the fact we can't buy clothes for our family's girls that doesn't seem to have pink in.

RT @mokuska: We lost R's hat so Ash chose a replacement, which she loved: blue, with a bear on. "From the boys' section?"

MT @alexlewispaul: We didn't know before birth, asked mother-in-law to knit with yellow/lilac/etc. Then random people were horrified re days-old boy in [them].

The significance we as a culture attach to colour is amazingly powerful and constraining, eh?

3rd December 2012

Lots of great presents here at towardthestars.com including an "I can rescue myself" princess t-shirt via

153

@GirlEmpowerment (in US). If you have tips for places to get Christmas presents that aren't steeped in pink and blue, please tweet us and we'll retweet for the benefit of all. We'll also do a blog rounding up places to buy presents that are gender-neutral.

5th December 2012

Did anyone notice the most ironic quote in this piece, *More Dads buy the toys, so Barbie, and stores get makeovers* (New York Times, 3rd December 2012)? " Barbies are for girls and construction sets are for boys. Or are they?" Consultant on Barbie, said adults had been a "limiting factor" in why girls have not played with those toys as often. *Hollow laugh*

10th December 2012

Ah yes, the Father Christmas boy/girl presents, I forgot this... Our pink-loving 5-year-old nephew and his sister were given toys labelled by gender. She was not remotely interested in her pink purse whereas he grabbed it and said "Wow let me see". Their younger brother left the toy car he was given at the next fair they went to. I'm bored of the assumption a child will like a toy you've chosen by gender.

15th December 2012

Our crowd-sourced list of where to buy gender-neutral presents for kids in @Bea_magazine:

(Blog reprinted here)

Presents of mind

If you're reading our blog, you know as well as us that products that are marketed to kids are frequently trying to put them into pink and blue straitjackets. Lots of you tweet us with awful examples of what is often the same thing packaged differently to reflect some supposed appeal to gender.

How did we get to this point? Indulge yourself with a browse through **pictures** of the 1976 Argos catalogue.[21] No really. There is almost nothing that is pink, even among the 'girls' toys. Likewise there are no pages of fierce, dark-coloured aggressive toys like those marketed to boys now. We'd love to write you a thesis on what happened in between now and then, it'd be fascinating. But frankly right now we just know we want this to stop. The message toy marketing is now sending our kids is that your gender defines what you play with. Hands up who wants their kids' play to be defined by their genitals? You neither?

So this month it's simple, a crowd-sourced list of places to buy presents that won't offend your sense of equality. Yes it may be a bit late for Christmas online ordering, but bookmark this page for future presents. You may be the only person who gives a child a non-gender conforming present, so your gift can be really important in showing them something different. Thanks to everyone who made a suggestion. They're mostly UK based with a US round up at the end.

Clothes

Tootsa MacGinty "are unisex clothes for children who want to step into a rainbow and splosh through the colours"

Love it love it love it, "colourful, comfortable and eco-friendly."

Toys

Myriad Natural Toys & Crafts, "Quality natural play products, toys, art and craft materials."

Orchard Toys, "Designer and manufacturer of award-winning children's games and jigsaw puzzles."

Ikea, "Great sturdy toys, not gendered, pics of boys and girls on the (minimal) packaging."

This is Wiss, "Original and stylish yet practical items for you and your little one."

Science Kits

Maplin, Electronics kits that, as pointed out by a follower, have boxes depicting girls and boys.

Curious Minds Science Shop, "A science, nature & technology shop for toys."

Books

Letterbox Library, "Celebrating equality and diversity in the very best children's books. We believe that challenging stereotypes and discrimination should play a fundamental part in every child's education."

And of course use our book list for great ideas for kids aged 0-14.

Films

Our film list of course.

USA

Really everyone should look at A Mighty Girl, "The world's largest collection of books, toys and movies for smart, confident, and courageous girls."

MindWare, "Brainy toys for kids of all ages."

aMuse Toys, "Well designed, creative toys that encourage children's development."

If you're feeling fired up about this then we can point you at a group campaigning specifically on this subject. Let Toys be Toys have been doing a great job of being seen out and about in the media and pointing out that toy marketing has become horribly restrictive. They have a petition you can sign.

That's an important campaign and we're right behind it, but something to point out is that it's very easy to get focused on toys and though it's important, we wouldn't want anyone to assume that toys becoming more gender-neutral would solve any of our greater sexist problems, really they're just a symptom of it. The example set by Sweden is that if you have a culture, and indeed a basis in law,[22] that is dedicated to equality for children then the elimination of this kind of harmful stereotyped marketing to kids will happen as a consequence of that, not the other way around. Shall we all move to Sweden? Or shall we change things where we are?

Diary continued

17th December 2012

Hasbro agrees to make a gender neutral Easy Bake Oven after a 13-year-old wages an online campaign. Sadly, the Easy Bake story reinforces the idea that boys cannot/should not like anything pink/purple. In this case the object is deemed to be OK for boys but the colour of it is not. That's a pretty weird culture we live in, right? And as always the fact a boy 'can't' like/own anything in purple or pink is because of its association with girls. Being like a girl=shame. I don't want to negate the Easy Bake story though because there are good intentions behind it. Gender-neutral toys are needed in our silly culture.

RT @ShelbyKnox: I would say to clarify that [the 13-year-old] was first concerned with having boys on the package and the media made it more about colors.

RT @ShelbyKnox: But you're right -- we teach boys that pink = girls, and girls = shameful, everything he should not want to be or be like.

Thanks for that, it's always useful to know the facts, and I think her aim and what she achieved is brilliant regardless.

18th December 2012

Do you prefer a boy or a girl? Yikes to this 'family balancing' in the news. It's tragic. The problem is that people have an assumption about what a child will be like based on their gender. That's so restrictive.

30th December 2012

Meant to say, this is ripe for satirical reviews like the Bic pens thing:

MT @jrwagz: What? Cutlery for boys? (Villeroy & Boch Play! for boys Children Cutlery Set 4pcs)[23]

5th January 2013

In Boots yesterday. Two shelves. 'Boys' toys' and 'girls' toys'. On the boys' side, science kits. On the girls side, Disney princesses.

12th Janury 2013

To the cinema this morning for the latest Tinkerbell movie. Dreadful film (obv), but refreshing to see so many female characters and decent ones too. We went to see the first one due to our rule that every second film our daughter sees should have a female lead. It's a tough rule to enforce, but Tinkerbell films are a pleasant surprise. Like the fact she's a tinker, which basically means an engineer. In fairy language.

14th January 2013

Thanks to everyone for lovely comments. We've tweeted as @GenderDiary for two years and the diary side of the account has dwindled recently and it feels like a good time for a little rest. But we'll still tweet and retweet when the mood takes. Or even be back with a vengeance soon if the fire is back in the belly. Here's the final reflective blog if you missed it:

(Blog reprinted here)

Terrible twos

This will be our last regular blog post for the foreseeable future and you may hear a bit less from us on Twitter. It's been liberating to write down thoughts and to have a forum where we can share ideas to help the problems with gender stereotyping kids. When we started tweeting we never imagined how much it would interest other people, how it would lead us to connect with some brilliant individuals and to learn from them. But after two years the cathartic method of using a diary format to tweet about the sexist treatment of our kids can feel repetitive. Not to mention it gets more complex as they get older.

Marianne Grabrucker's diary was for the first three years of her daughter's life. Our children are 5 and 2 now. Her diary ends quite abruptly and you can almost sense her exasperation with what she has recorded but also that she's returning to work, and life must move on.

Before moving on, a little flashback five years – Gender Diary-mum is laid low with post natal depression, health problems, breastfeeding nightmares and lack of sleep. All these things compounded a furious and righteous anger that dawned during maternity leave. We, who had been the most equal of partners, found ourselves in a situation where financially (due to the construction of our society) it was only possible for the woman to stay at home – even if she didn't want to. It brought us both back to an engagement with feminism because, selfishly, now we needed it so much. We still do. We all do. But this might be a slightly indulgent way of explaining something about the recent online arguments about intersectionality. Cariad Martin wrote a blog that borrowed the old Tony Benn idea about leaving the House of Commons to devote more time to politics –

she said she was intending to devote less time to discussing feminism (or watching on the sidelines as others fought wildly), and more time to doing feminist things. The discussion and debate that goes on online is incredibly important, and different people are at different points in their uh, for want of a better phrase, feminist journey. Intersectionality makes perfect sense, but right now debating it at length is not where we're at, personally. More and more one half of @gendediary looks at Twitter and feels depressed again. Marianne Grabrucker went back to her job as a lawyer and got her diary published – that's modelling the alternative to the things in society you don't like. More of that later.

In all our blogs we promised a split between moan and solution which was done with these issues in mind. This blog ought to be no different, so finally here are some of the things we've learnt from tweeting, blogging and being parents.

The most important one we've learnt is to go easy on ourselves. The pressures of pink princess culture for girls and the rejection of anything 'girly' for boys is difficult for children to resist. We do what we can to fight against it, but we try never to blame ourselves or feel guilty about the fact that our kids buy into it. We'd drive ourselves to distraction otherwise.

We try never to force our opinions on our kids but we also don't feel guilty for wanting them to become feminists. When some rail against those parents who have the intention of bringing up their children as 'gender-neutral' they complain they are brainwashing their children, as though other parents are imposing nothing of their ideas on their children. Children are very much a product of their parents engineering, even if that is not intentional.

Likewise, we don't feel guilty for wanting our children to share our views on equality when toy companies are pushing gender stereotypes and have multimillion pound budgets that are intended to influence kids way more than parents do. As we've shown in other blogs, we bring books, films, toys and attitudes into our house that reinforce our ideas of equality and we're proud of it.

As Marianne did, we've done what we can to model the alternative to society's stereotypes in our house. We've shaken up our roles where they were typical. We weren't in a position to make use of shared parental leave (which we hope will eventually be improved), but if you are, give a lot of thought to how you use it. Rebecca Asher's book *Shattered* is well worth a read on how and why parental leave is vital to furthering equality. She also shows that if both parents take that leave they are then more inclined to split the childcare on a return to work. We both work a short week. It works for us. Times are hard and choices are always fewer during economic difficulties. That thing from before about not feeling guilty applies here too. And everywhere.

In other simple ways we have made changes to the way we do things. This will sound horribly politically correct but we aim to take it in turns to drive so we don't fall into our parents' model of Dad always driving whenever he's present because the car is his domain. It's a simple thing. There are lots of those.

And remember you're not alone. For all its faults Twitter has been an invaluable source of support, encouragement and sisterhood/brotherhood. We didn't start tweeting with an end in mind but it's been delightful and empowering to learn there are so many like-minded folk out there not just talking the talk but walking the walk and standing up, speaking out and taking inspiring actions to make things better for our daughters and sons.

It's been a privilege to be a part of it.

Afterword

Two years have passed since we finished writing diary entries on a regular basis and though we ended it on a bit of a down note, there is much to be pleased about.

For example the publisher Usborne confirmed they will no longer publish books 'for boys' or 'for girls'. Boots, Debenhams and Center Parcs stopped using 'boy' and 'girl' on their toy signage. This work was down to one of the excellent new campaigns to emerge in the past two years – Let Toys Be Toys. Other notable activism that has popped up includes work by Girl Guiding, Water Aid's #Tobeagirl campaign, and the incredible Malala Yousafzai's Malala Fund. We noted the attempted murder of a girl in Pakistan towards the end of the diary, and in the short time since, Malala has become a global phenomenon and inspiration to us all.

Meanwhile feminism in popular culture has also changed. There is a lot less shuffling of feet when people describe themselves as one. In 2014 Beyonce broadcast to millions with the word FEMINIST emblazoned in 10 foot high letters behind her.

Whether you count this the third, fourth or fifth wave of feminism is immaterial, what matters is that current activism does constitute a wave with all the power and irresistible force that implies. The feminist tide has risen higher since our first child was born. An idea that's seeped everywhere from the glamour of a pop queen's stage set to the mundanity of a family holiday village can justifiably claim to have become part of the mainstream agenda. We're pleased there have been some changes, but there is still much to do.

References

[1] *A very sexist Christmas and a happy new year*, The Crafty Bat, 5th October 2011.
http://thecraftybat.blogspot.co.uk/2011/10/very-sexist-christmas-and-happy-new.html

[2] *Under-representation of females in pre-school children's television*, Dr Helen Mott.
http://k003.kiwi6.com/hotlink/7c4k4qwzvd/Nov08HMCBeebies Presentation.pdf

[3] *Baby Boy? Baby Girl? Baby X!*, Neurotic Physiology, 9th March 2011.
http://scientopia.org/blogs/scicurious/2011/03/09/baby-boy-baby-girl-baby-x

[4] *When did Girls Start Wearing Pink?*, Smithsonian.com, 7th April 2011.
http://www.smithsonianmag.com/arts-culture/when-did-girls-start-wearing-pink-
1370097/?onsite_source=smithsonianmag.com&onsite_campaign=photogalleries&onsite_medium=internal&onsite_content=When+Did+Girls+Start+Wearing+Pink%3F

[5] *Adventures from the frontline: running my first anti-sexism workshop with young children*, HatBlueMilk, Hoyden About Town, 31st July, 2011.
http://hoydenabouttown.com/2011/07/31/adventures-from-the-frontline-running-my-first-anti-sexism-workshop-with-young-children/

[6] *One teacher's approach to preventing gender bullying in the classroom*, Together for Jackson County Kids, Melissa Bollow Tempel, 16th December 2001.
http://togetherforjacksoncountykids.tumblr.com/post/14314184651/one-teachers-approach-to-preventing-gender

[7] *Invisible or involved fathers? A content analysis of representations of parenting in young children's picture books*, Adam, Matthew, Walker, Carl and O'Connell, Paul (2001), School of Applied Social Science, University of Brighton.
http://eprints.brighton.ac.uk/8145/

[8] *Gender Stereotypes and Representation of Female Characters in Children's Picture Books*, Kelly Crisp Paynter, Liberty University, October 2011.
http://digitalcommons.liberty.edu

[9] *Disney Princesses, Deconstructed*, Lisa Wade, Sociological Images, The Society Pages, 25th October 2009.
http://thesocietypages.org/socimages/2009/10/25/disney-princesses-deconstructed/

[10] *Changing the Game for Girls*, Women's Sport and Fitness Foundation, 2012.
https://www.womeninsport.org/wp-content/uploads/2015/04/Changing-the-Game-for-Girls-Policy-Report.pdf

[11] *Women's judo: It's disturbing to watch these girls beat each other up*, Andrew M Brown, The Daily Telegraph, 2nd August 2012.
http://blogs.telegraph.co.uk/news/andrewmcfbrown/100174361/womens-judo-its-disturbing-to-watch-these-girls-beat-each-other-up/

[12] *On the Olympics, sports in schools and new female role models*, Carried Dunn, Bea Magazine, 13th August 2012.
https://beamagazine.wordpress.com/2012/08/13/on-the-olympics-sports-in-schools-and-new-female-role-models-by-carrie-dunn/

[13] *Thanks (but no thanks…)*, Zoe Pablo Smith, 23 July 2012.
https://zoepablosmith.wordpress.com/2012/07/23/thanks-but-no-thanks/

[14] *Abuse in Rochdale: brutality meets a blind eye*, The Guardian, 27th

September 2012.
http://www.theguardian.com/commentisfree/2012/sep/27/abuse
-rochdale-brutality-blind-eye

[15] *Pakistani girl shot over activism in Swat Valley, claims Taliban*, Jon
Boone, The Guardian, 9th October 2012.
http://www.theguardian.com/world/2012/oct/09/pakistan-girl-
shot-activism-swat-taliban?CMP=twt_gu

[16] *Male and female teachers' evaluative responses to gender and the implications
of these for the learning environments of primary age pupils*, Christine
Skelton and Barbara Read, International Studies in Sociology of
Education, Volume 16, Issue 2, 2006.
http://www.tandfonline.com/doi/abs/10.1080/096202106008498
02

[17] Adventures from the frontline: running my first anti-sexism
workshop with young children, Blue Milk, 31st July 2011.
https://bluemilk.wordpress.com/2011/07/31/adventures-from-
the-frontline-running-my-first-anti-sexism-workshop-with-young-
children/

[18] *One teacher's approach to preventing gender bullying in a classroom*,
Melissa Bollow Temple, Together for Jackson County Kids, 16th
December 2011.
http://togetherforjacksoncountykids.tumblr.com/post/143141846
51/one-teachers-approach-to-preventing-gender

[19] *The Extinction of Masculine Generics*, Brian D Earp, Yale University,
Department of Cognitive Science, 2012.
http://jcc.icc.org.ro/wp-
content/uploads/2012/05/JCC_vol2_no1_Brian_Earp_pages_4_
19.pdf

[20] *Response from Hasbro*, Jennifer O'Connell, 16th November 2012.
http://www.byjenniferoconnell.com/2012/11/update-response-
from-hasbro.html?m=1

[21] *Vintage British Argos 1976 Catalogue*, Anthony Voz, Flickr, 28

December 2008.
https://www.flickr.com/photos/38301877@N05/3589276287/in/set-72157619071382653/

[22] *Gender Equality in Sweden*, the Swedish Institute.
https://sweden.se/society/gender-equality-in-sweden/

[23] *Villeroy and Boch 1264142091 4-Piece Play for Boys Children Cutlery Set*, Amazon.co.uk.
http://www.amazon.co.uk/Villeroy-Boch-1264142091-4-Piece-Children/dp/B0089C79GY/ref=sr_1_8?s=kitchen&ie=UTF8&qid=1356883059&sr=1-8

Made in the USA
Charleston, SC
21 February 2016